This Book Belongs To:

____

Squirrels scamper and play,
storing acorns for a cozy day.

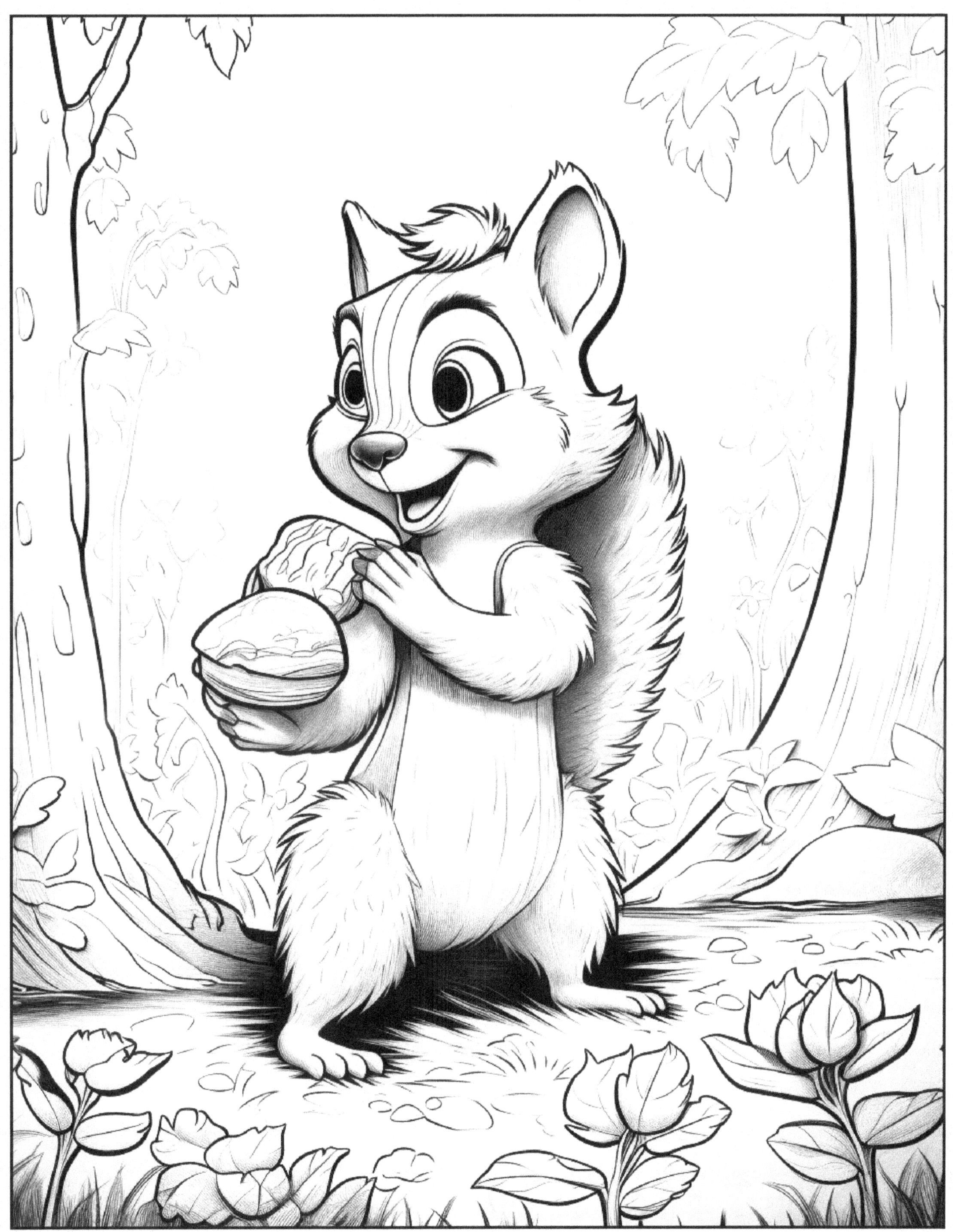

Hedgehogs curl up tight,
cozy and warm in the starry night.

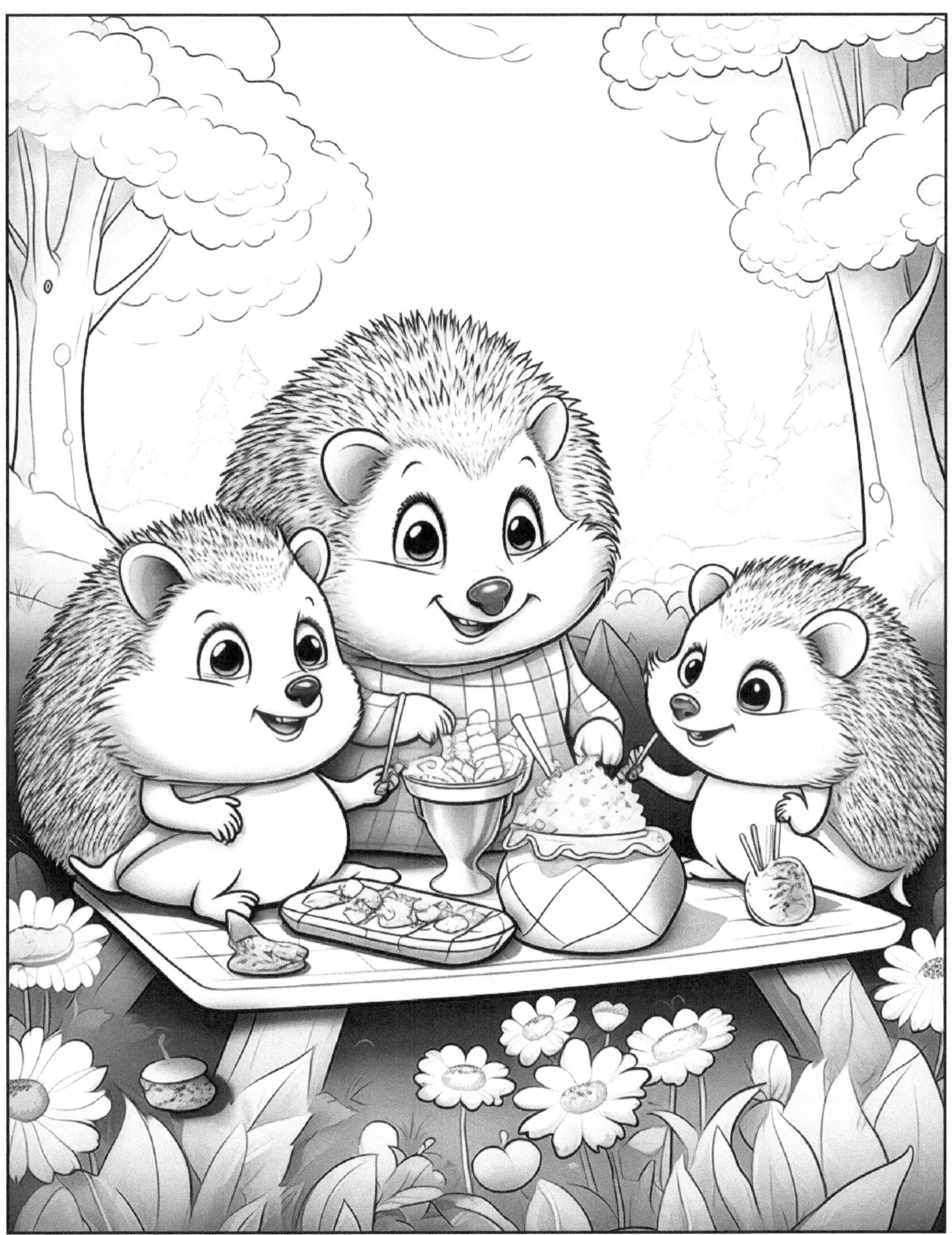

Owl in the night, wise and bright,
spreading calm with silent flight.

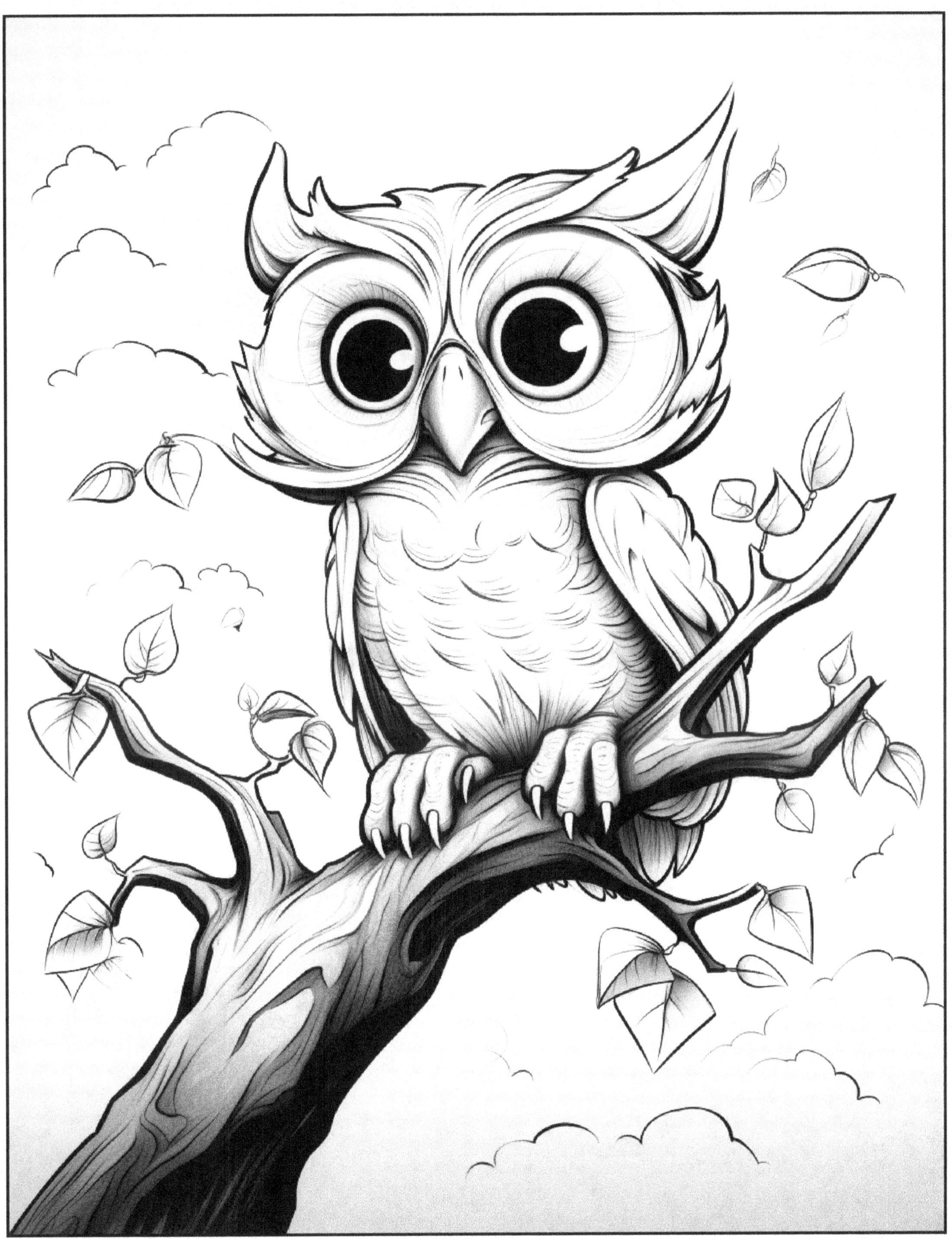

In a flower town, fairies twirl,
casting magic in a colorful swirl.

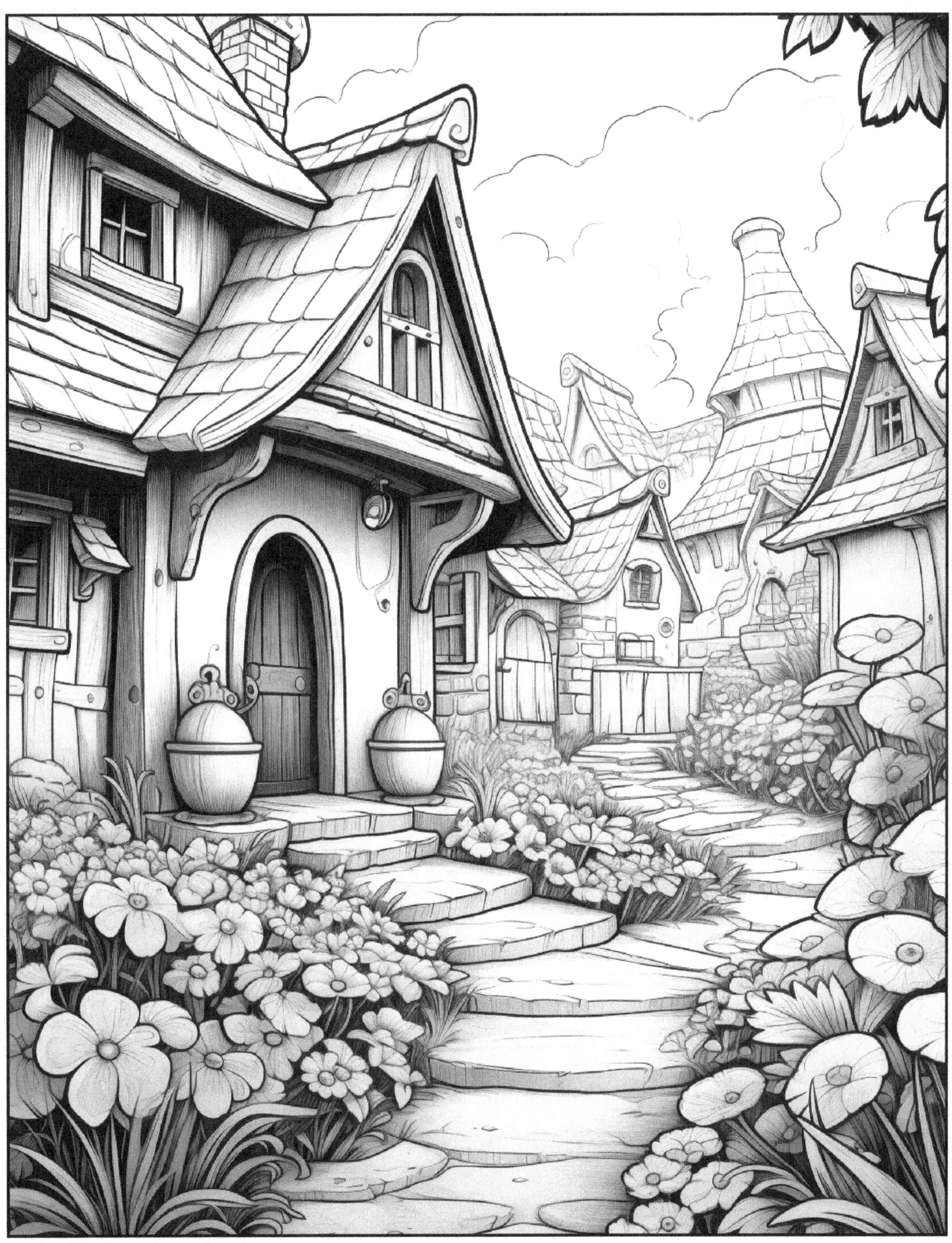

Frog leaps with glee,
hopping from pad to pad, dancing in
the marshy jubilee.

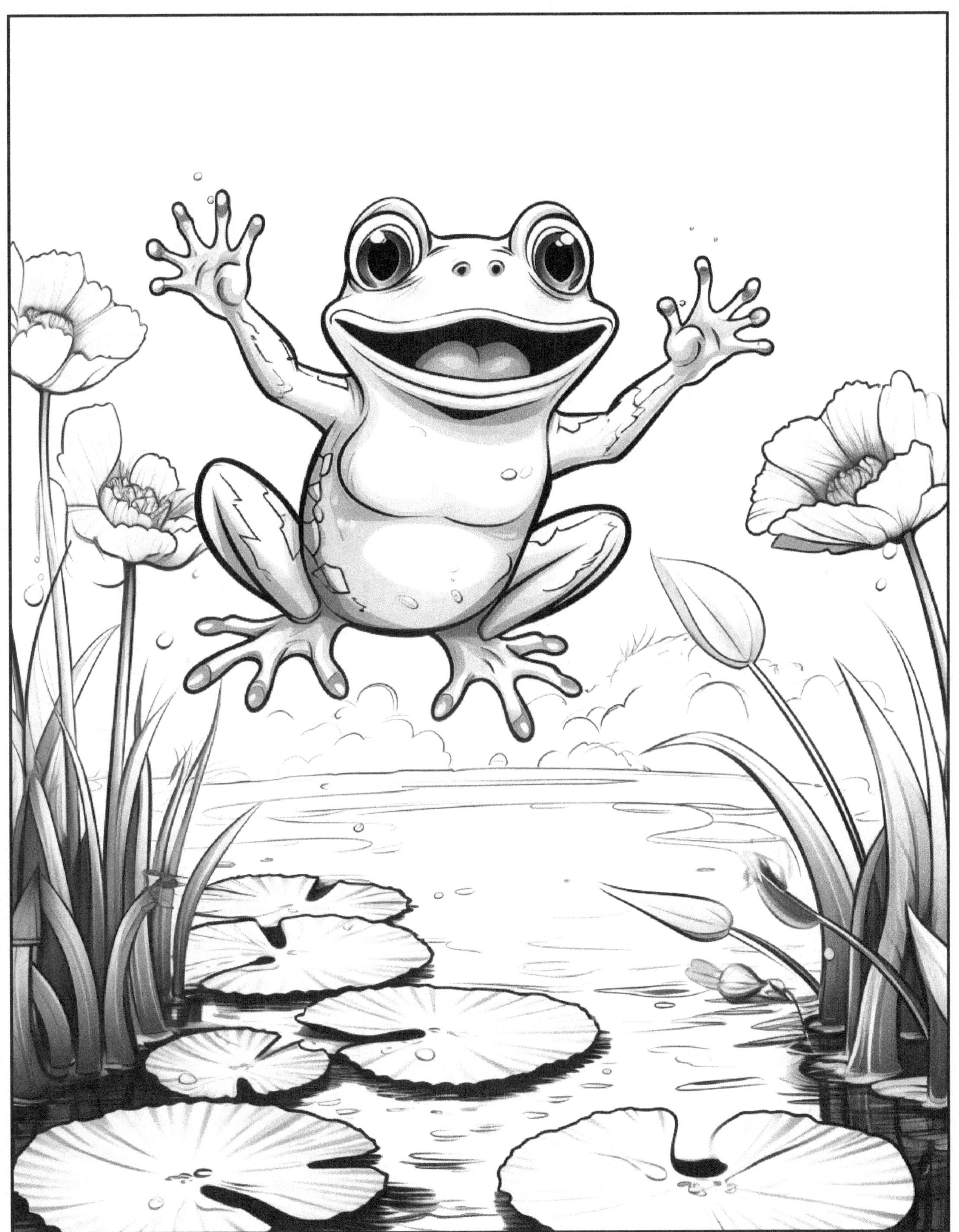

Waterfall dances down, a sparkling gown, nature's magic, all around.

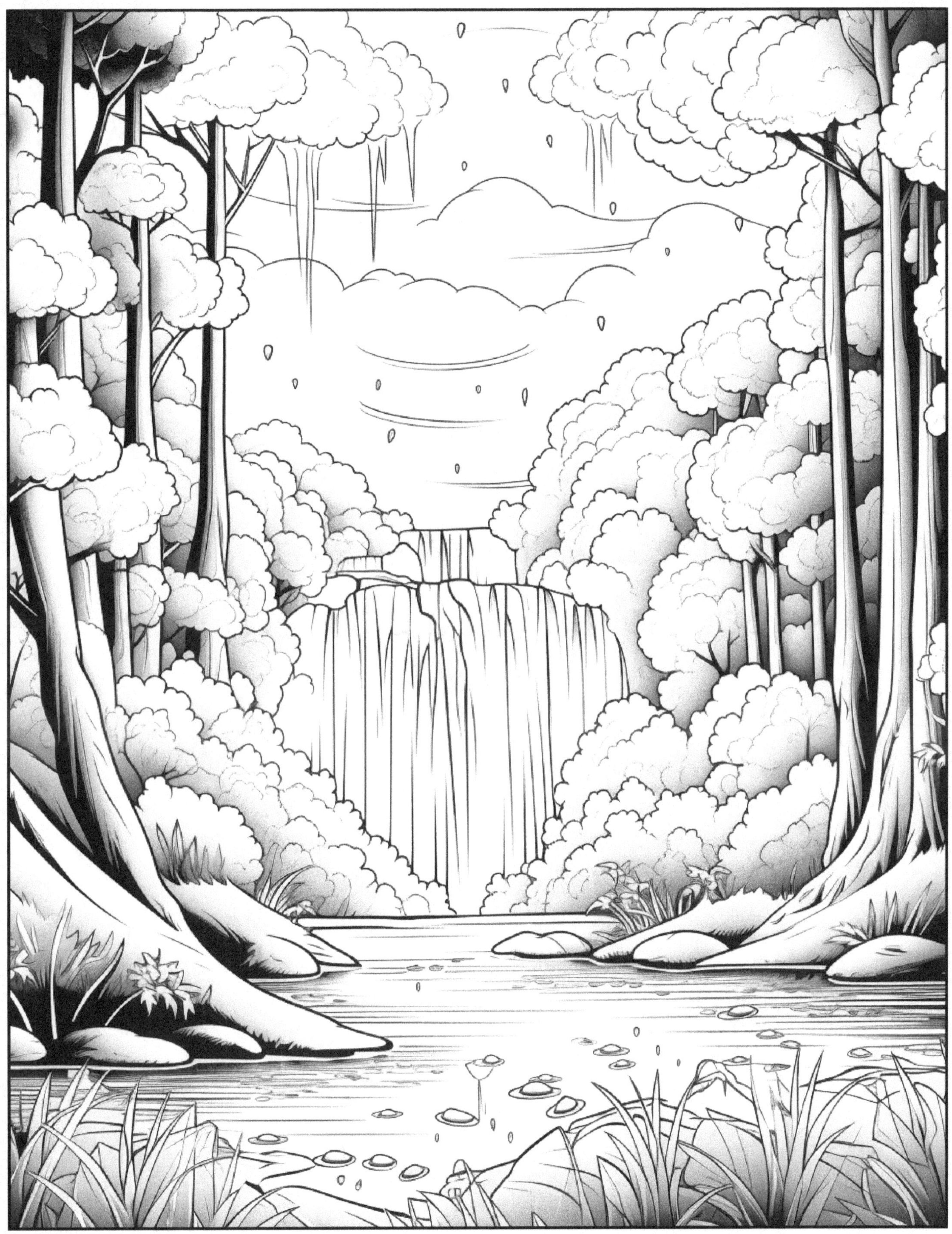

Deer with antlers tall,
a woodland king in a peaceful forest
hall.

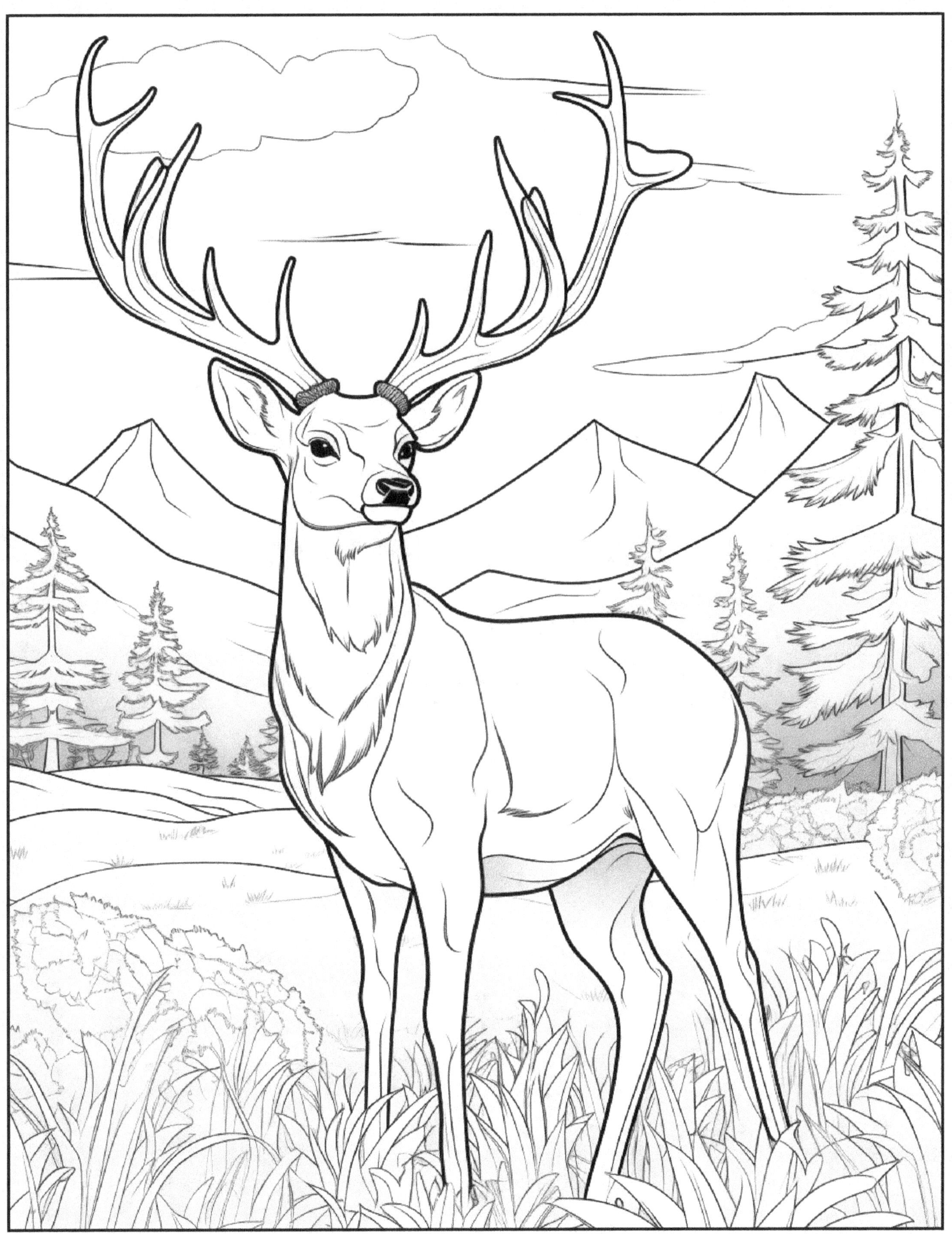

Butterflies take flight,
colors bright,
dancing in the sunlight.

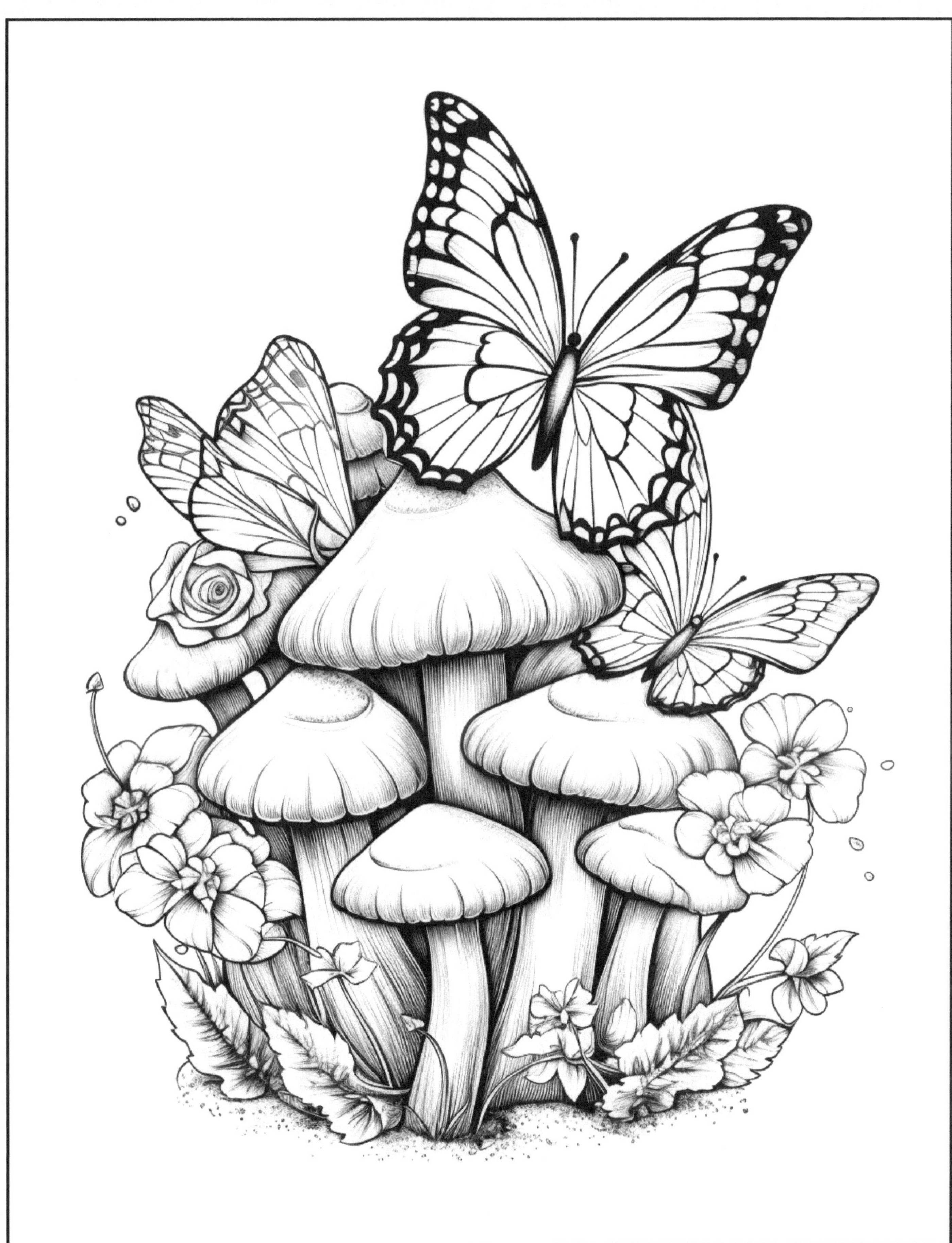

Raccoon on the prowl, curious and sly,
searching for treasures nearby.

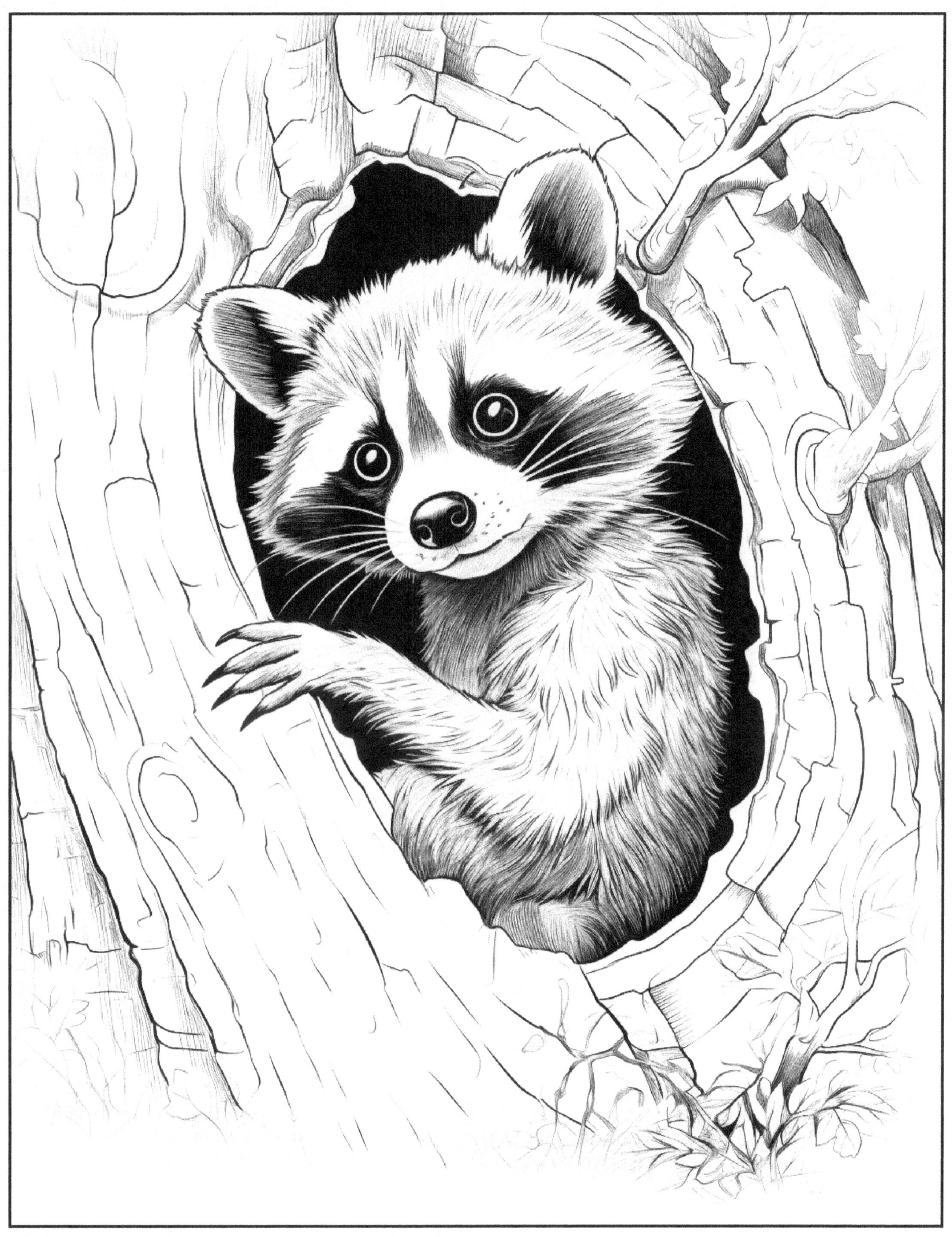

Pond so clear and blue,
home to turtles and frogs too.

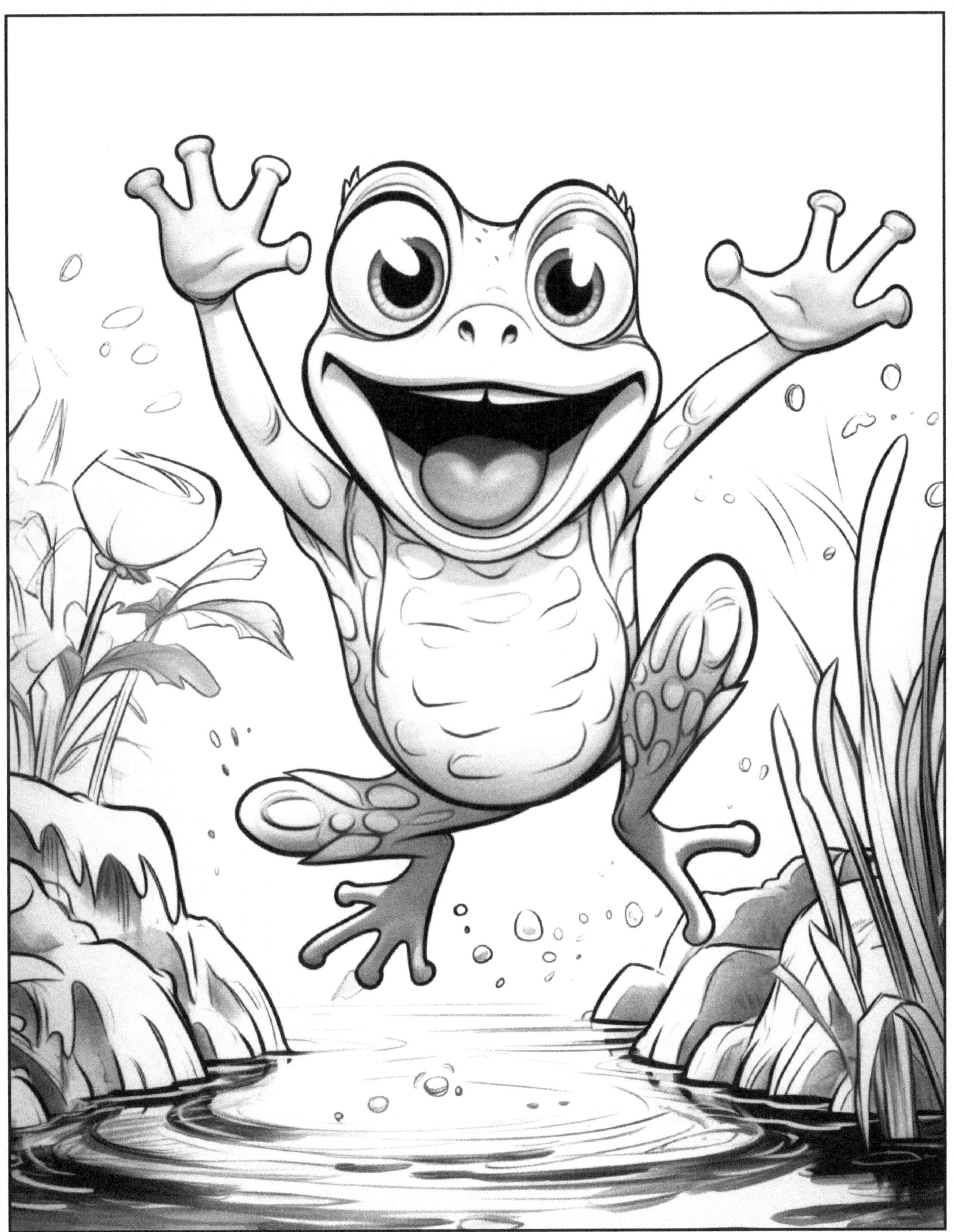

Bear by the brook, fishing for a treat,
a family day so sweet.

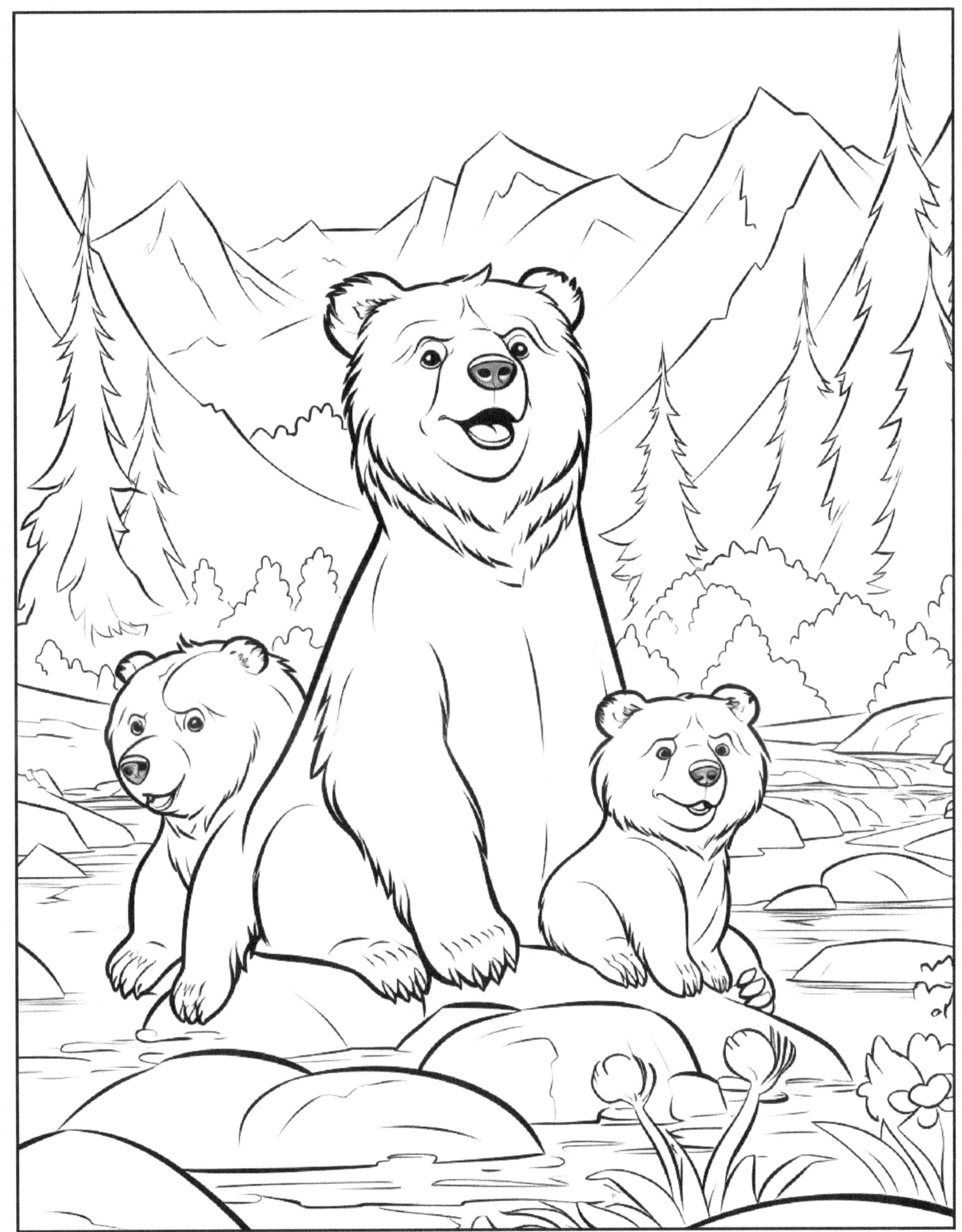

Wooden bridge so wide,
inviting us to the other side.

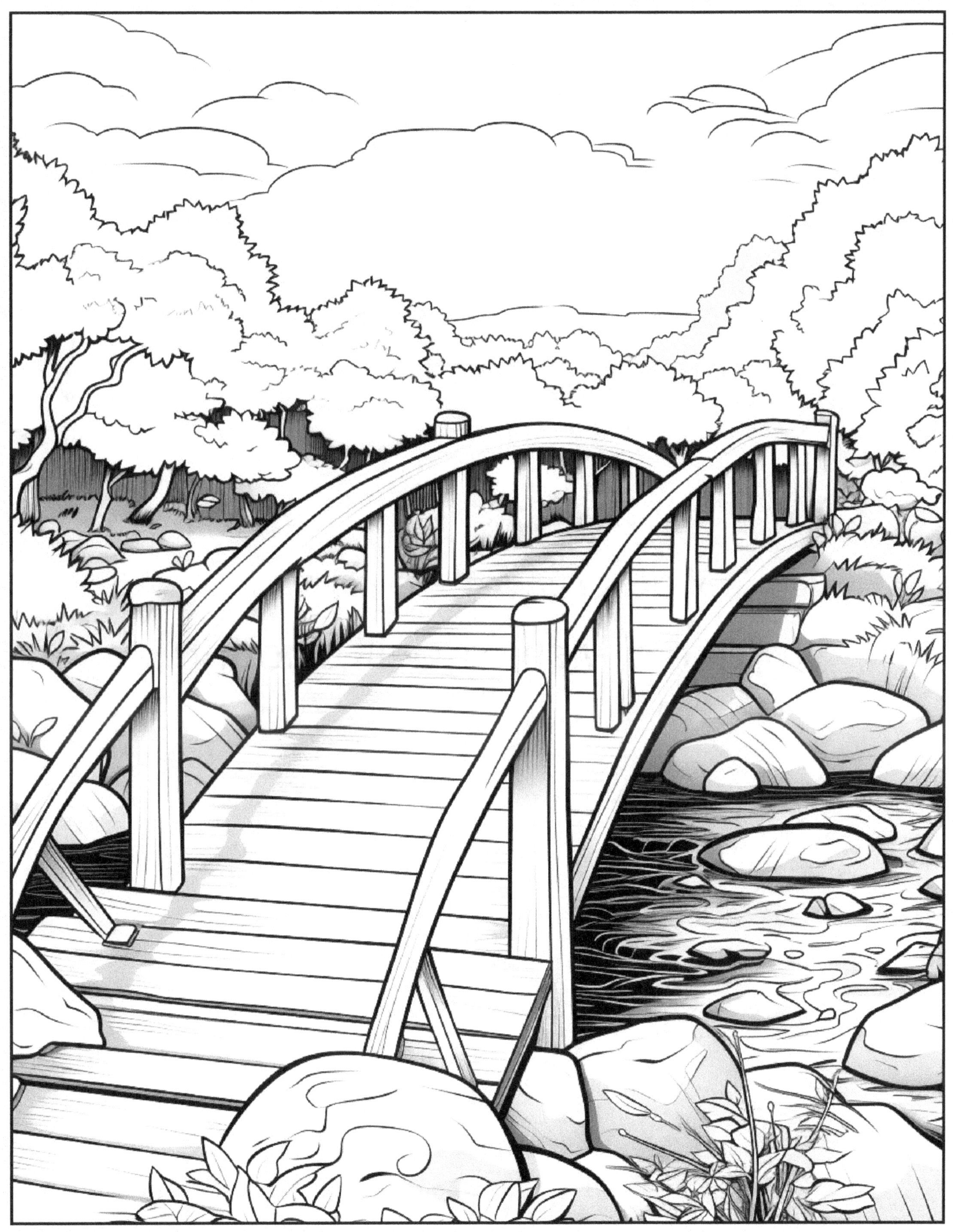

Magical well so round,
make a wish, joy will abound.

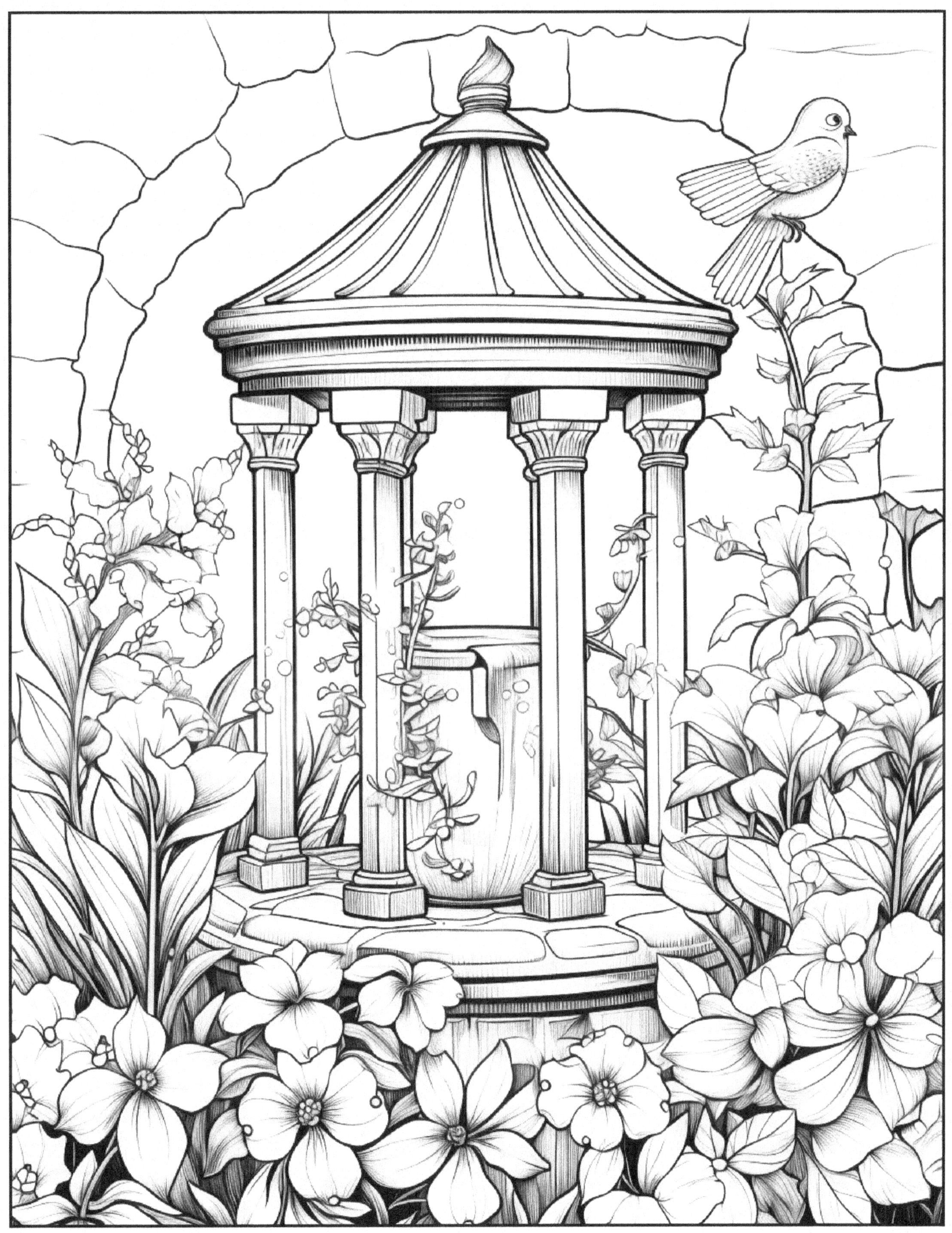

Otters in a line,
sliding down so fine,
laughter echoes in the woodland shine.

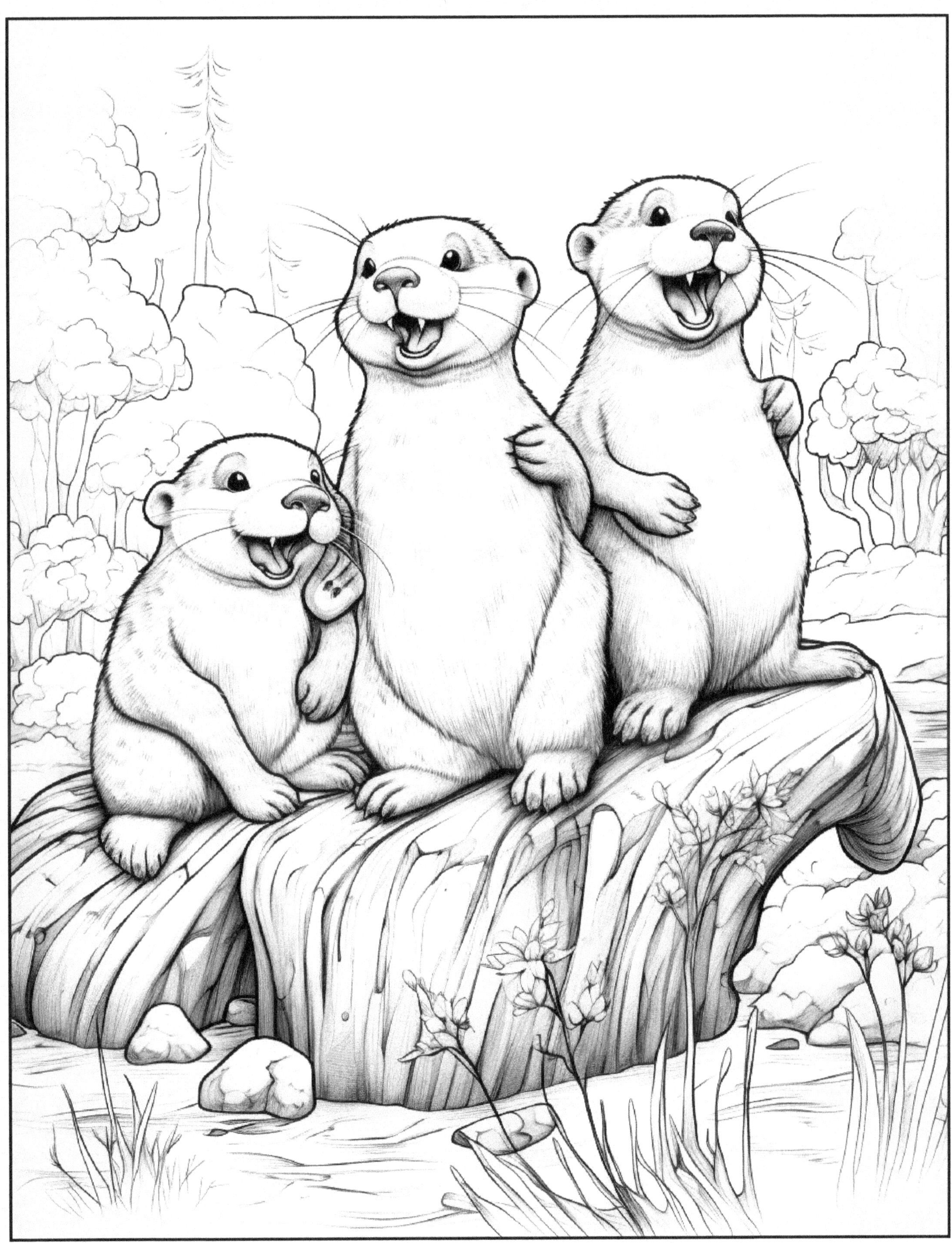

Chipmunks in a race,
sharing an acorn space,
a tasty treat, a happy chase.

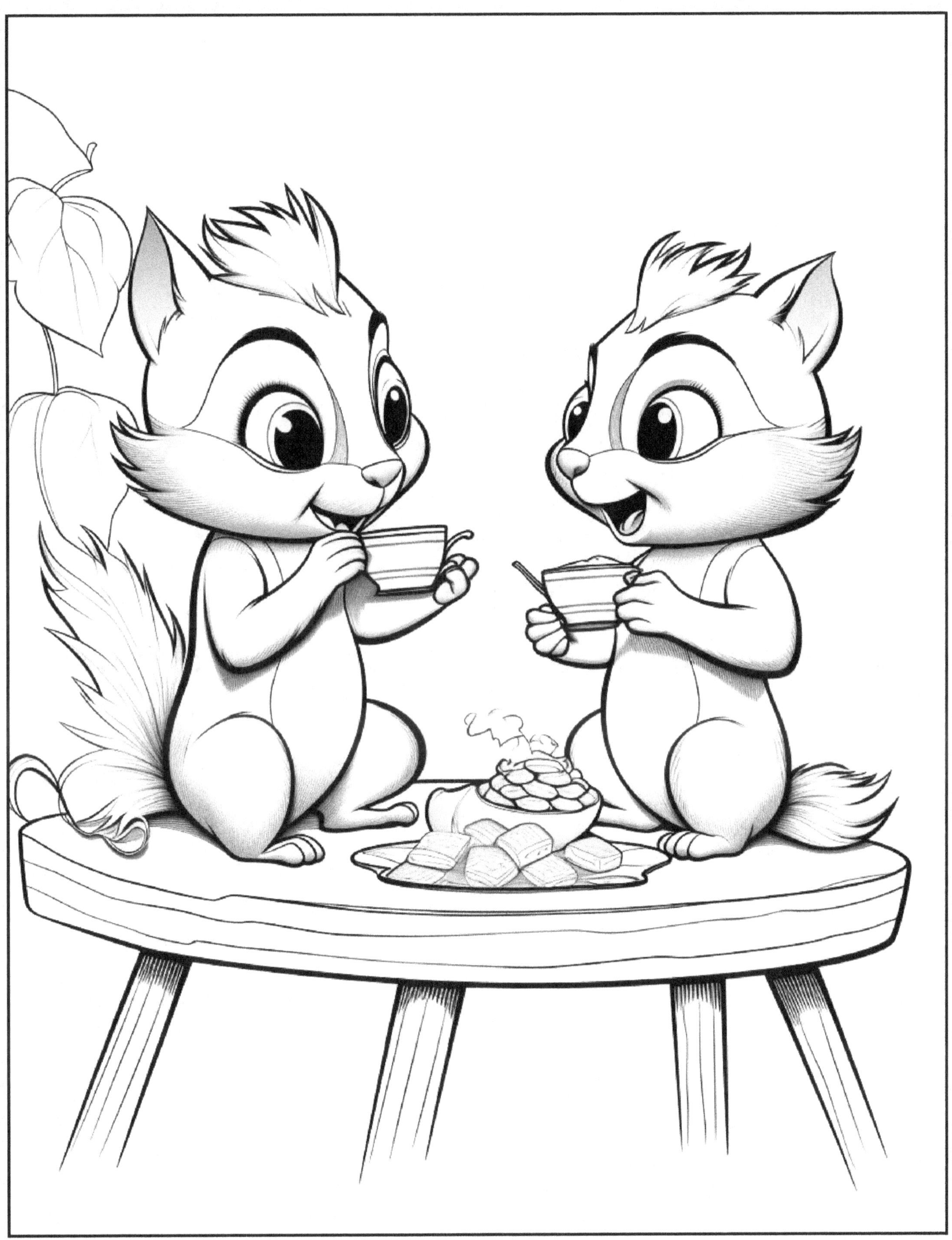

Dragonfly in the air,
wings so light, dancing without a care

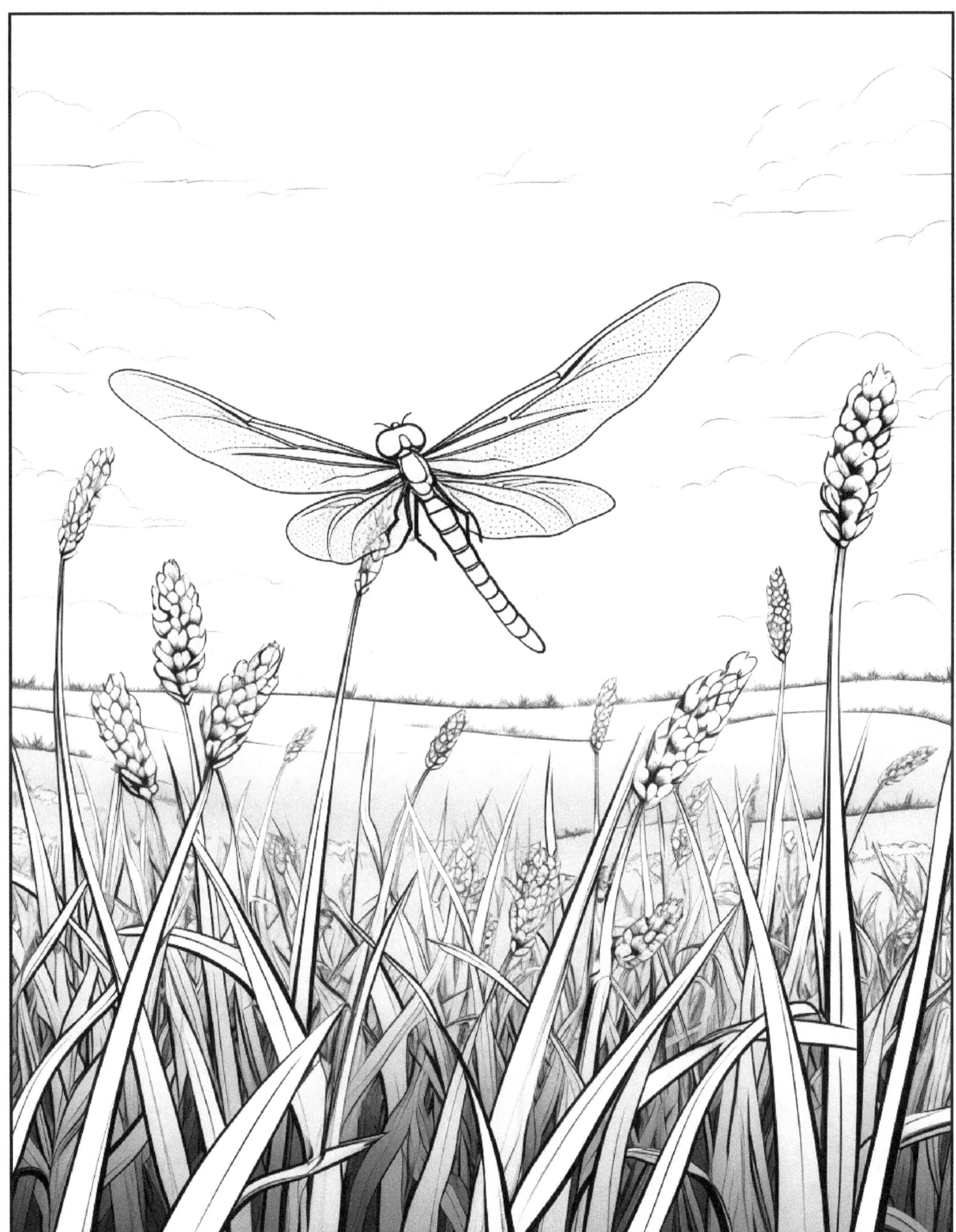

Leaves of red and gold,
autumn's magic to behold.

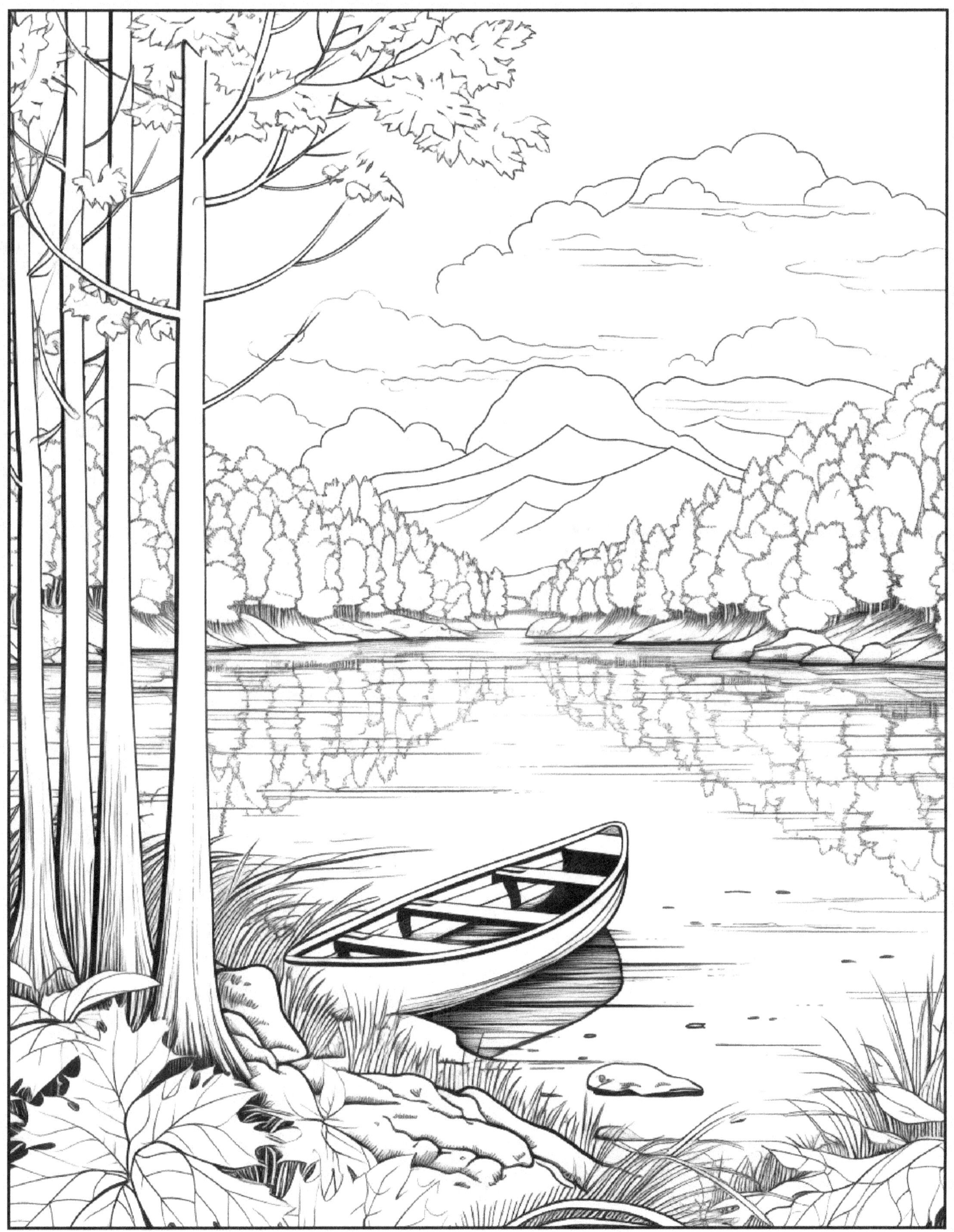

Birds in the trees,
singing melodies,
nature's joyful harmonies.

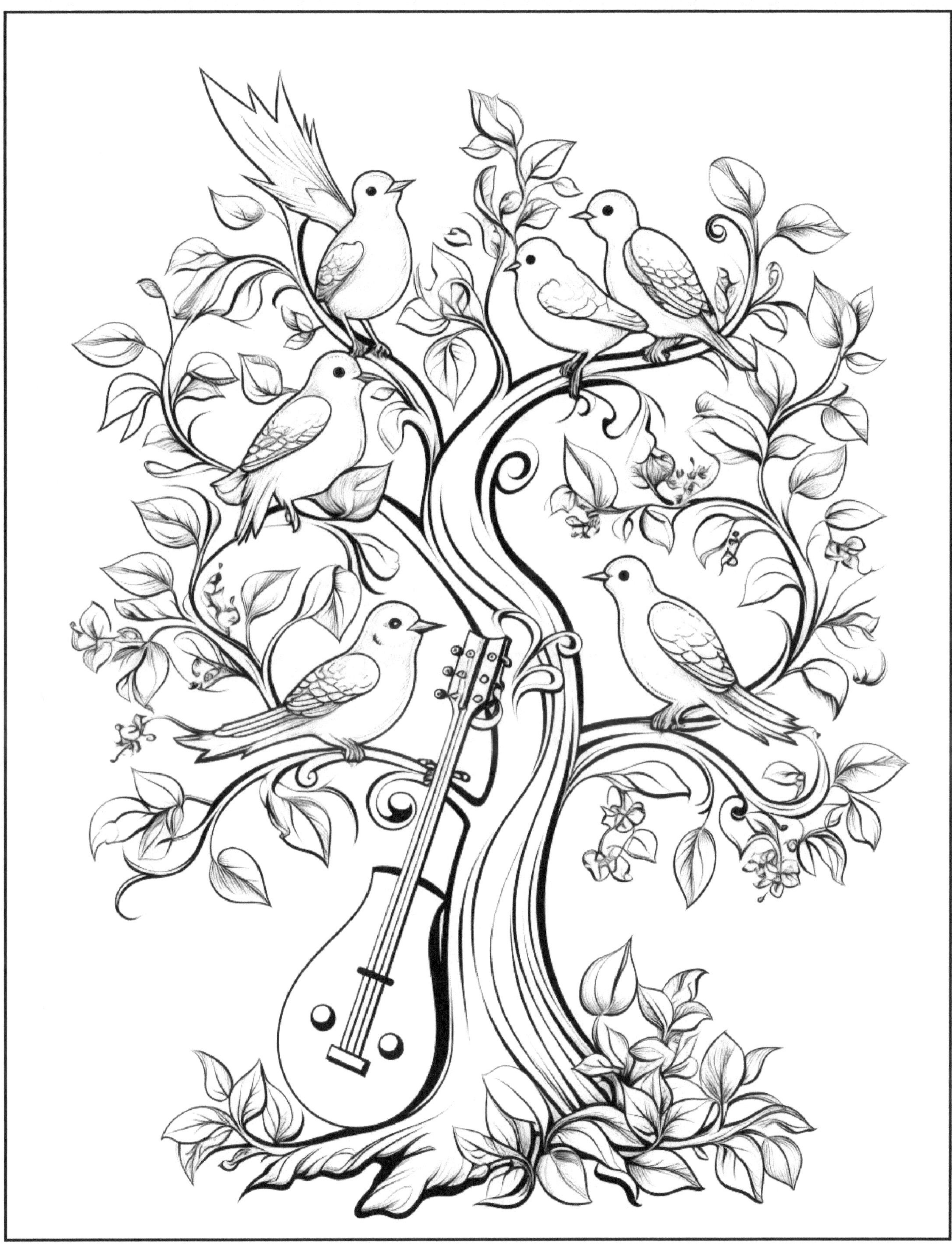

Treehouse in the tree,
a magical place for you and me.

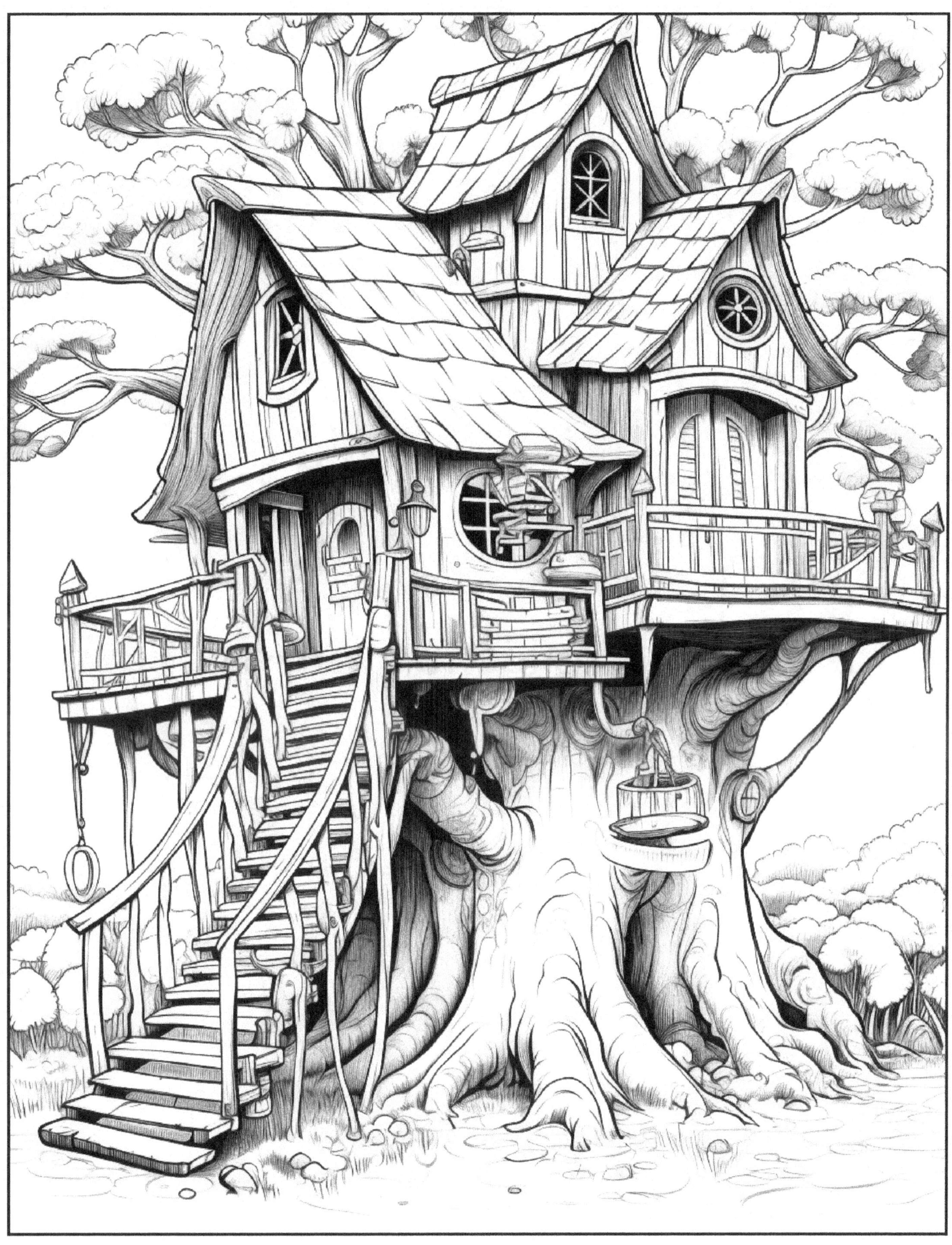

Fawn so small and shy,
discovers its reflection with a curious
eye.

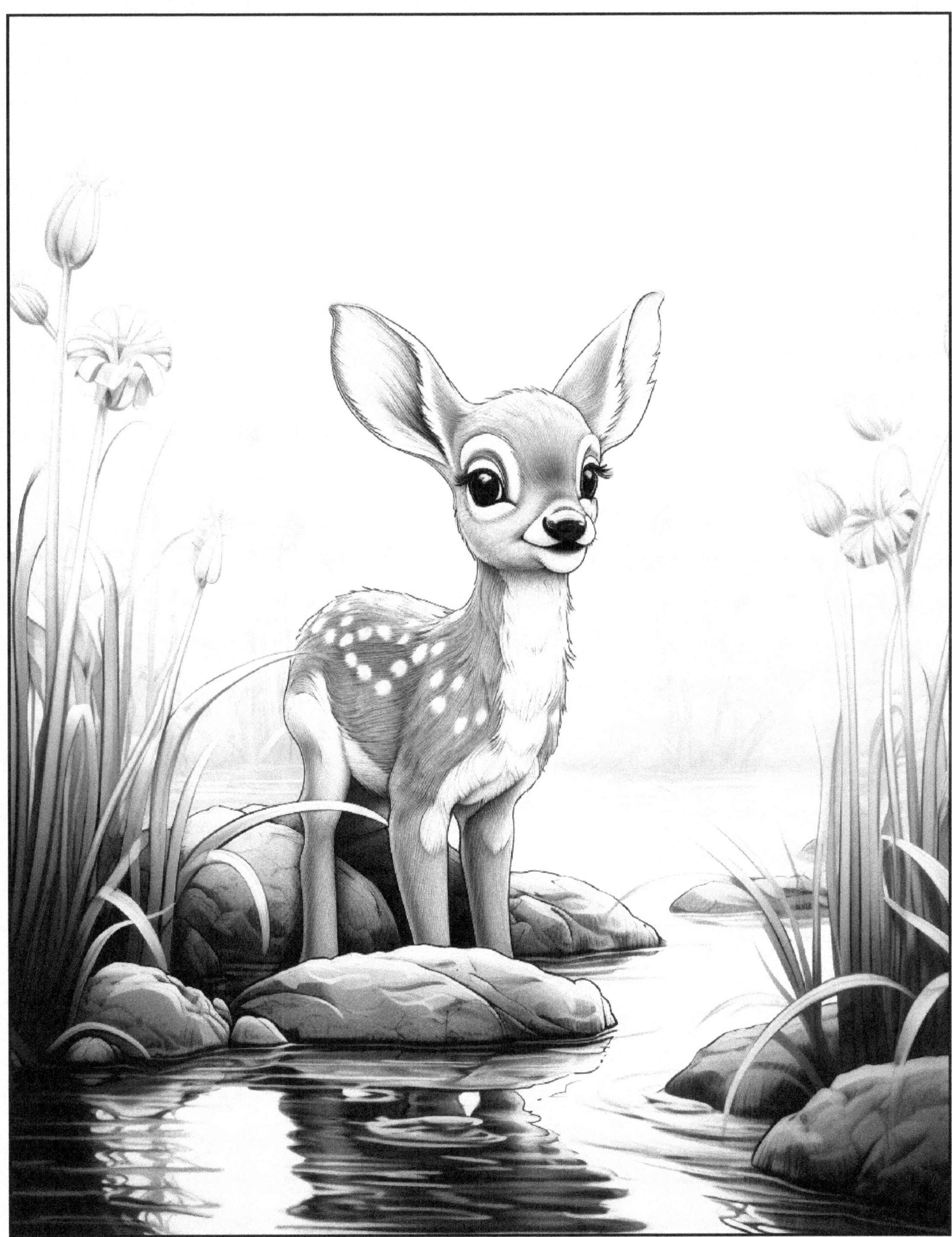

Fireflies light the way,
a glowing path to play,
in the woods, we'll sway.

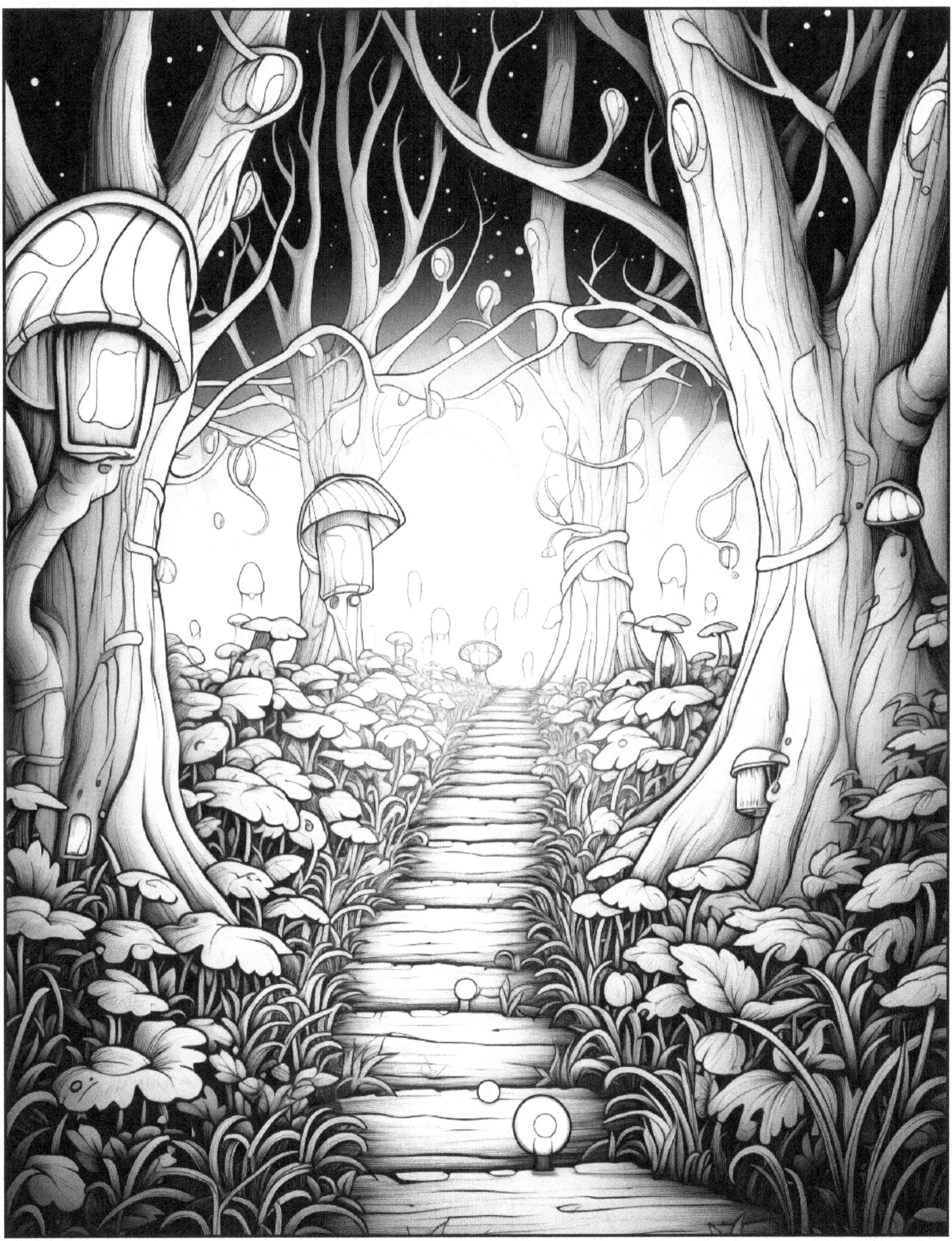

Unicorn in the meadow,
a magical dream to follow.

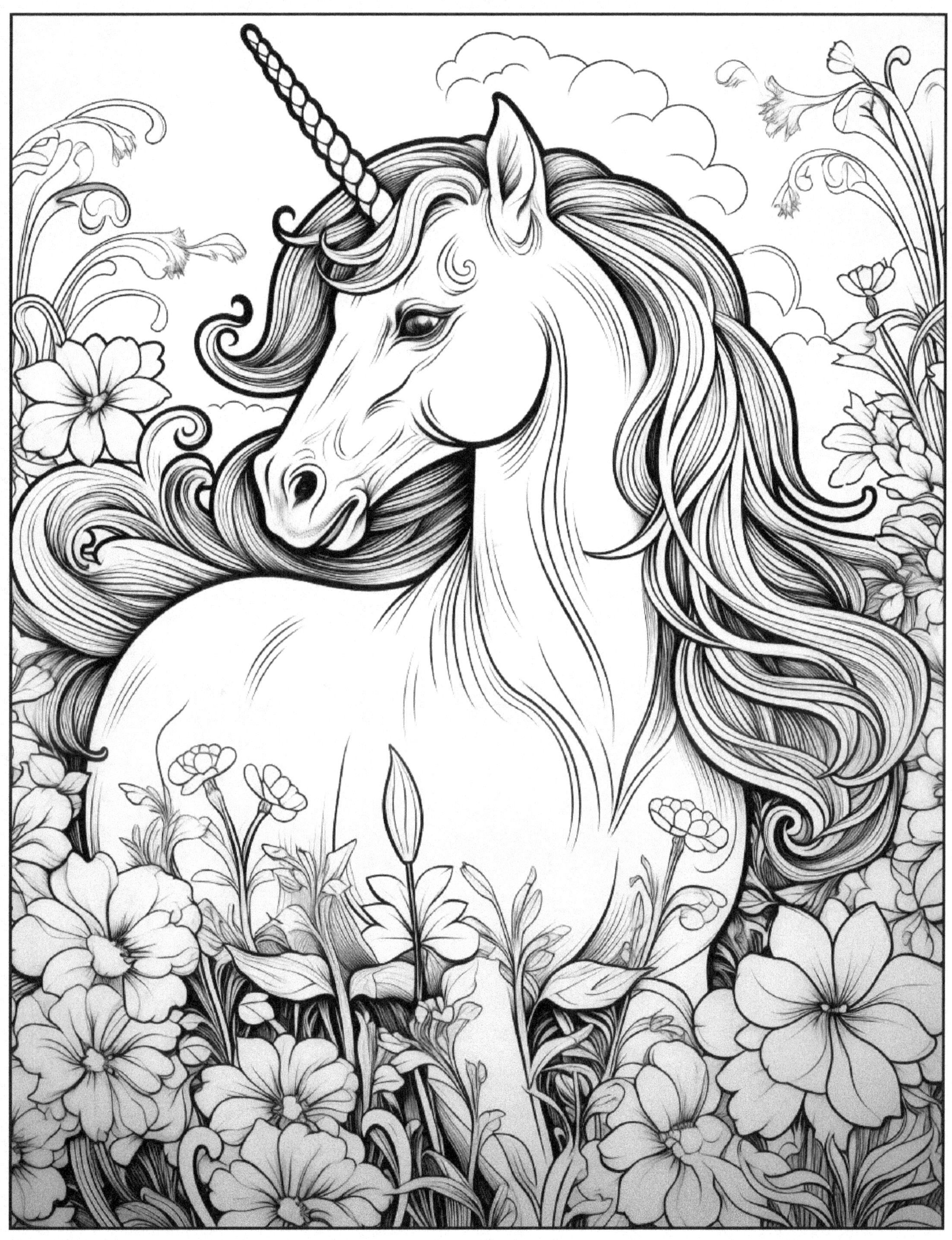

Wise old tree,
with eyes that see,
guarding the forest, happy and free.

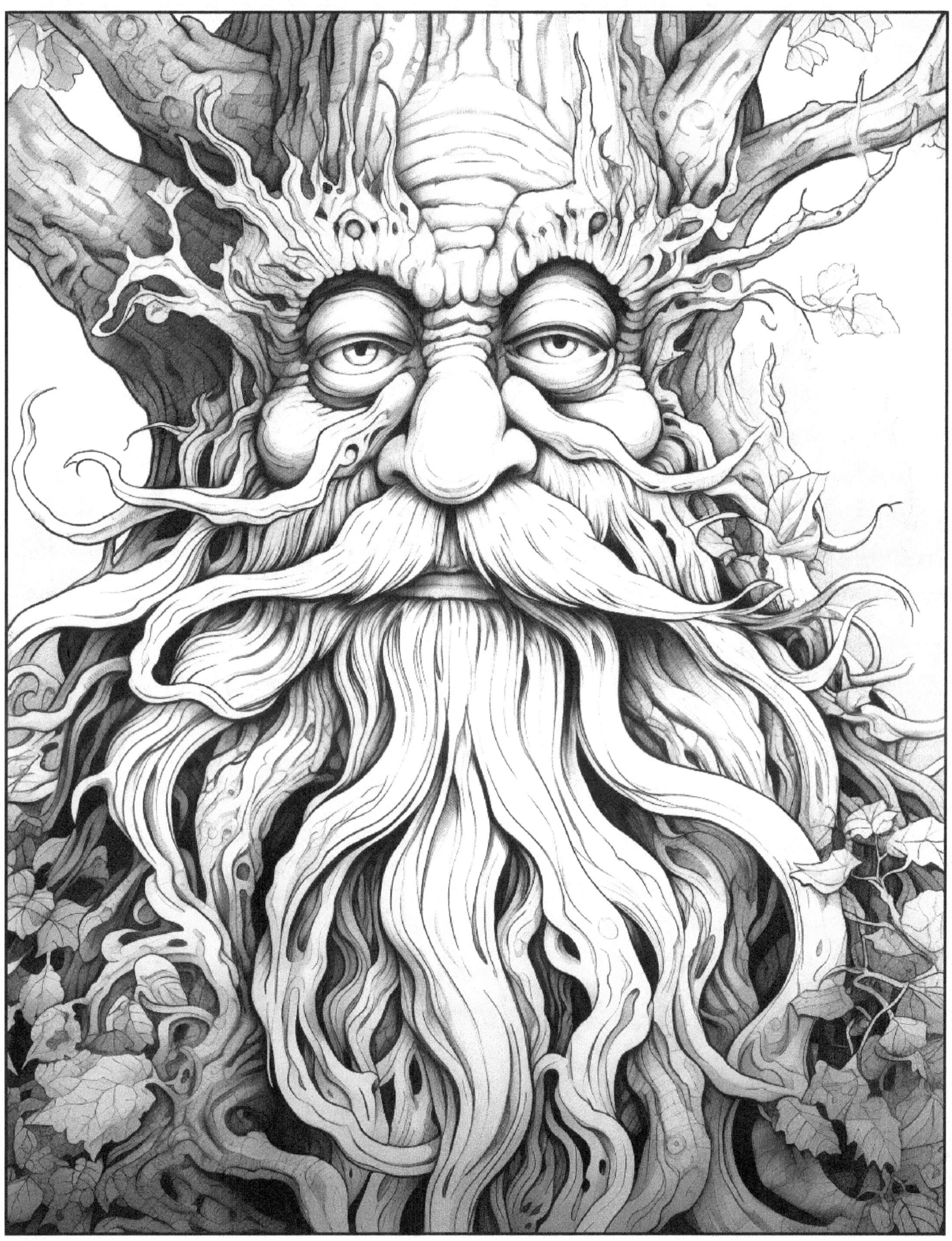

Busy beaver with a plan,
building a dam,
nature's engineer, so grand.

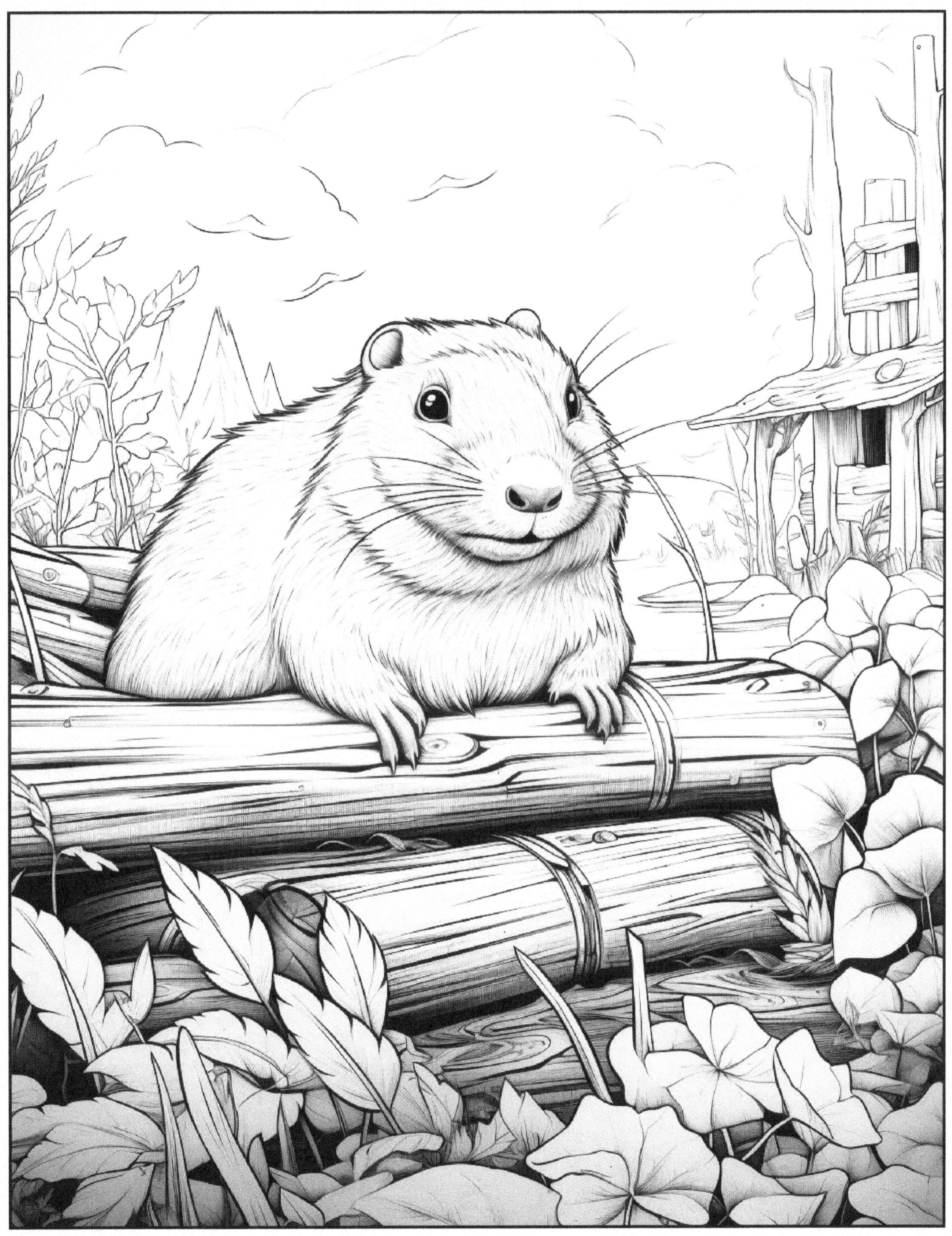

Turtles on a log, basking in the sun,
a turtle family having fun.

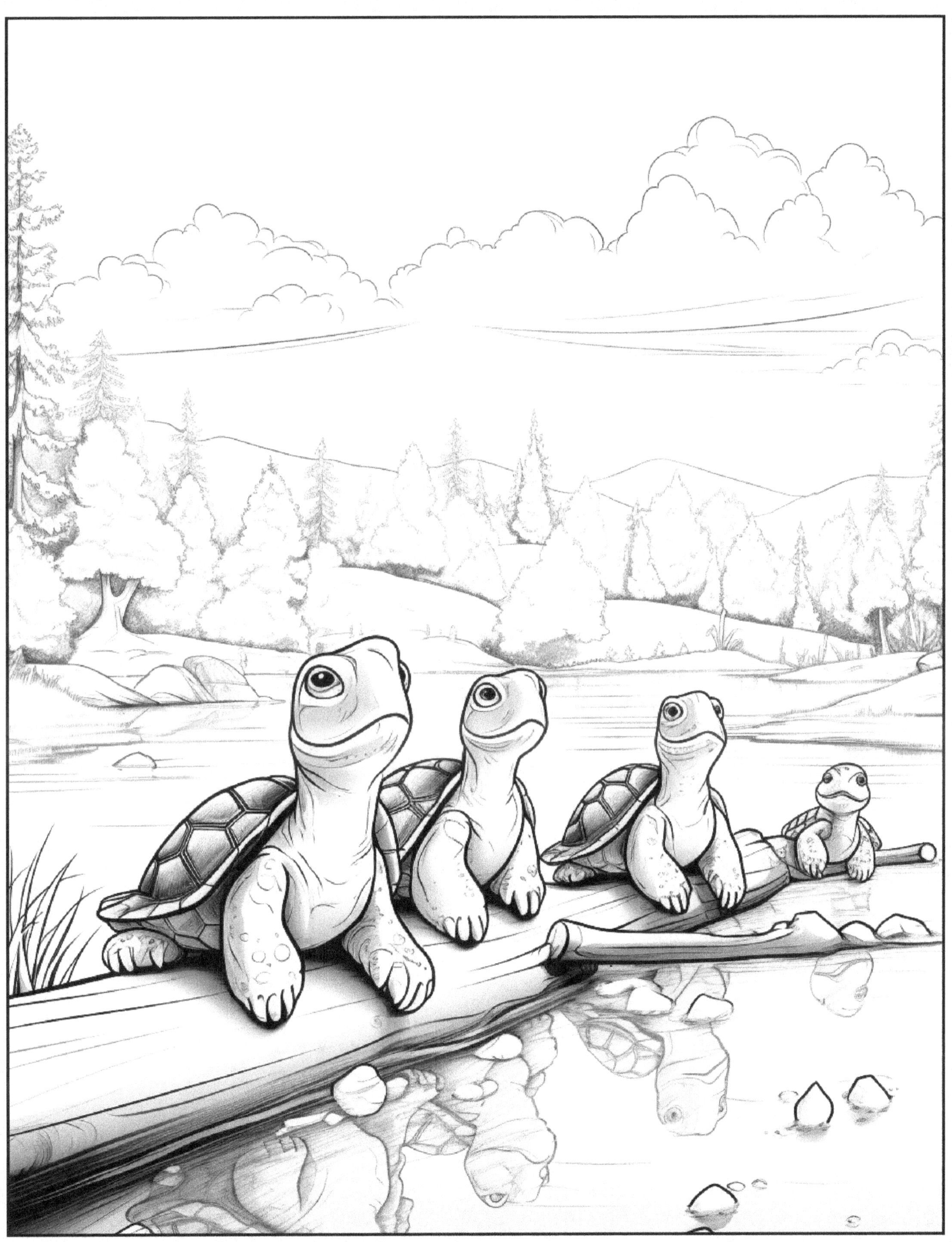

Gnome on a toadstool,
a little friend so cool,
in the woods, where dreams rule.

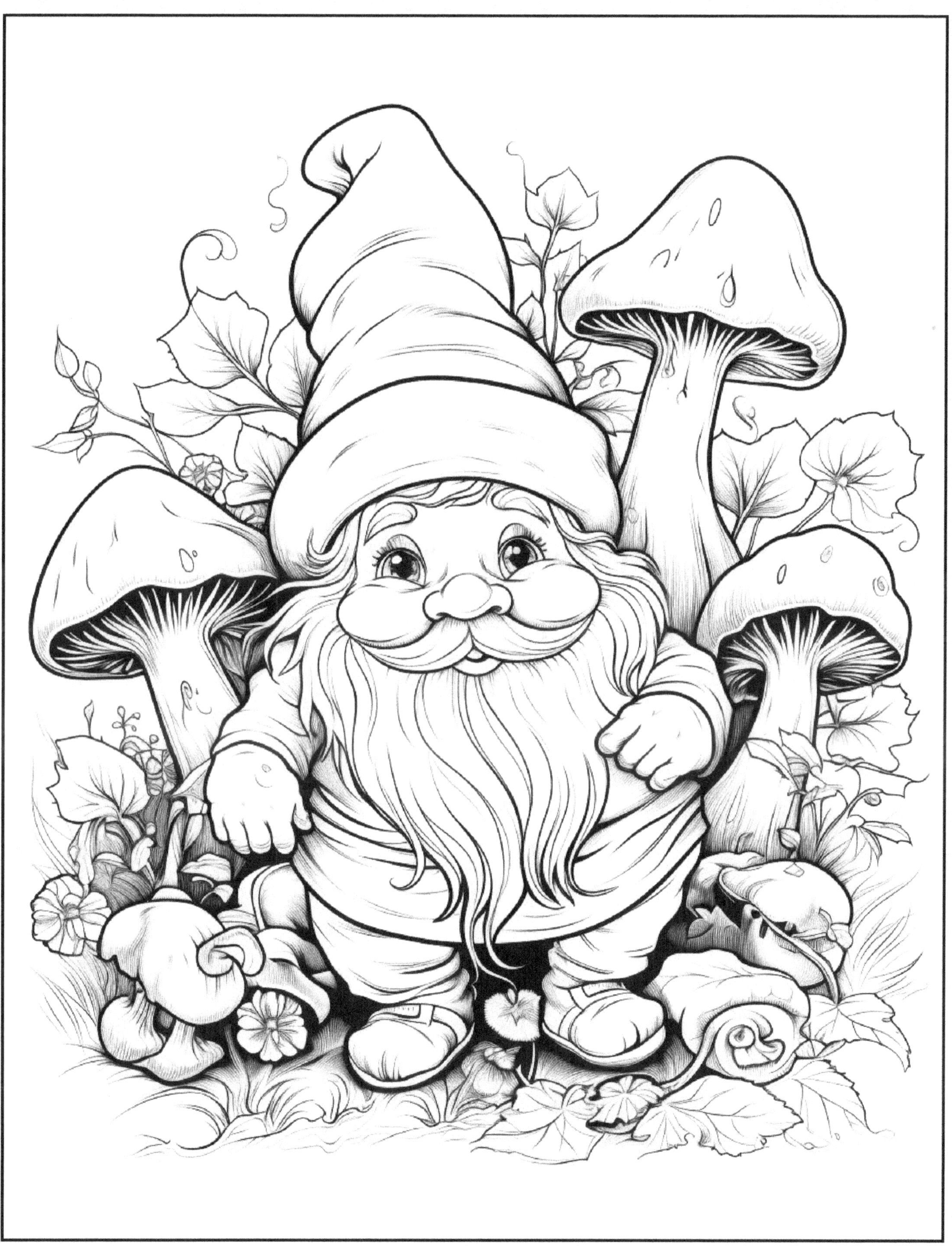

Bunnies in a dance,
under moonlight's trance,
a joyful hop, a furry prance.

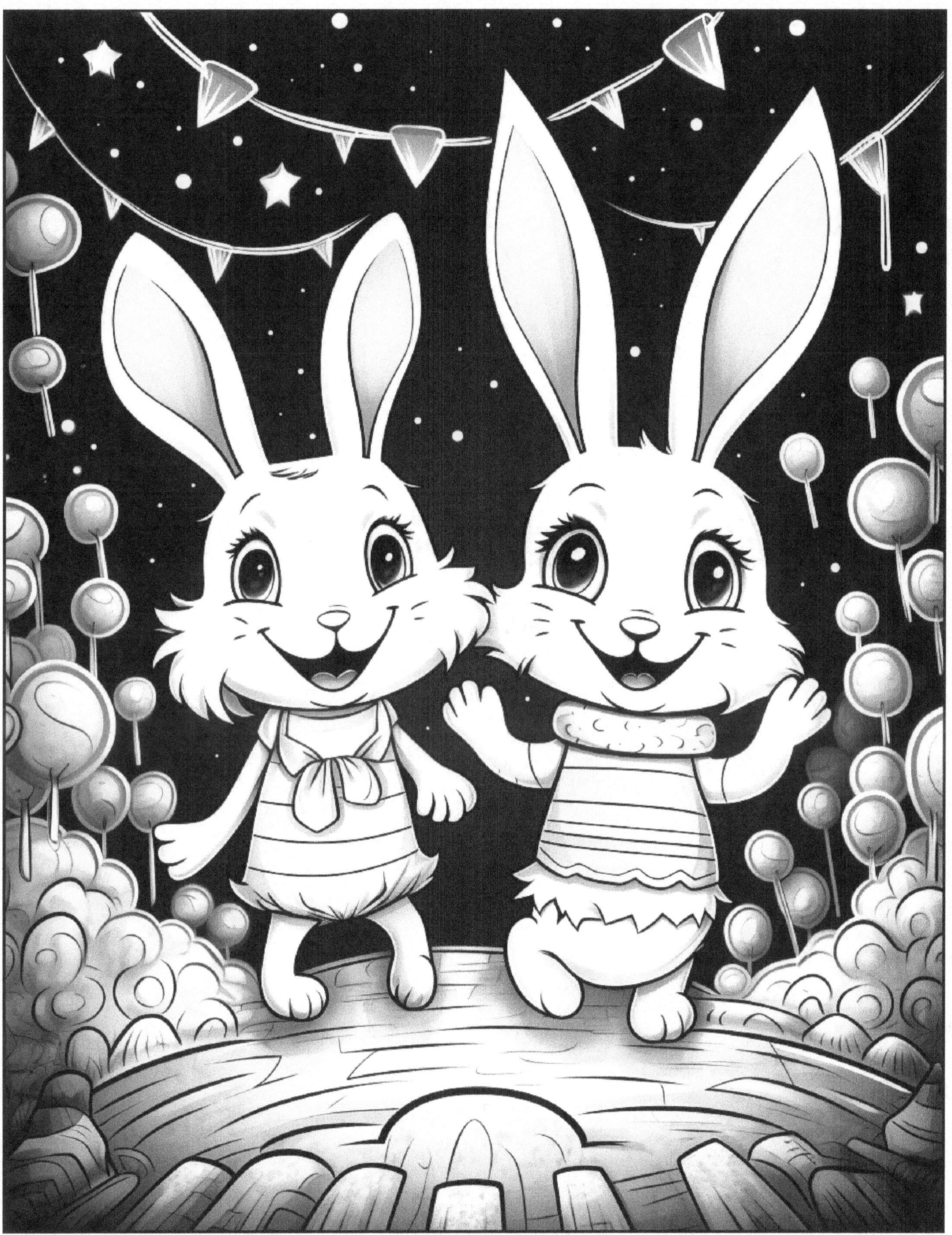

Caterpillar so small, transforms into a
beauty,
a butterfly in glee.

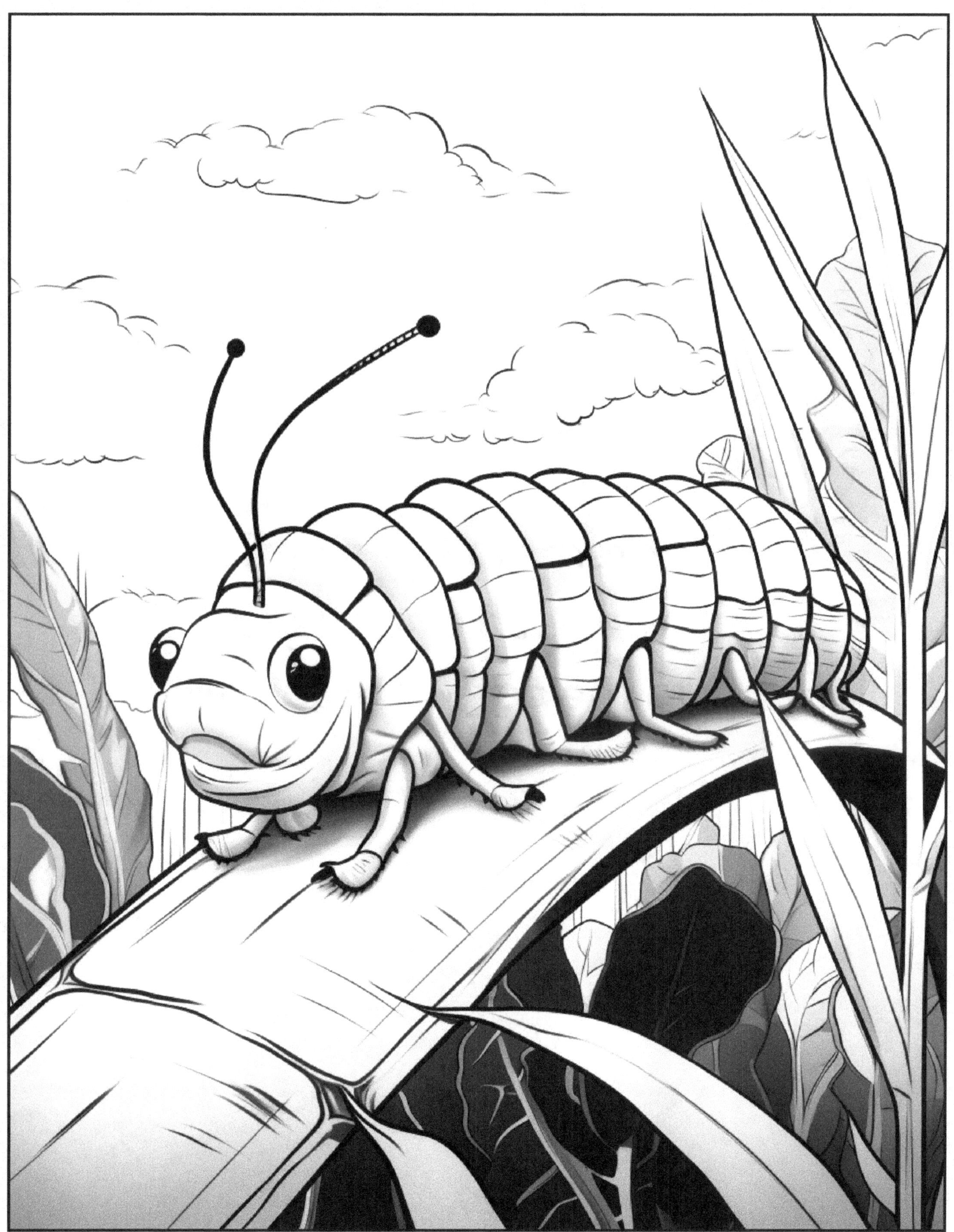

Lanterns in the night,
glowing soft and bright,
lighting up the path, a magical sight.

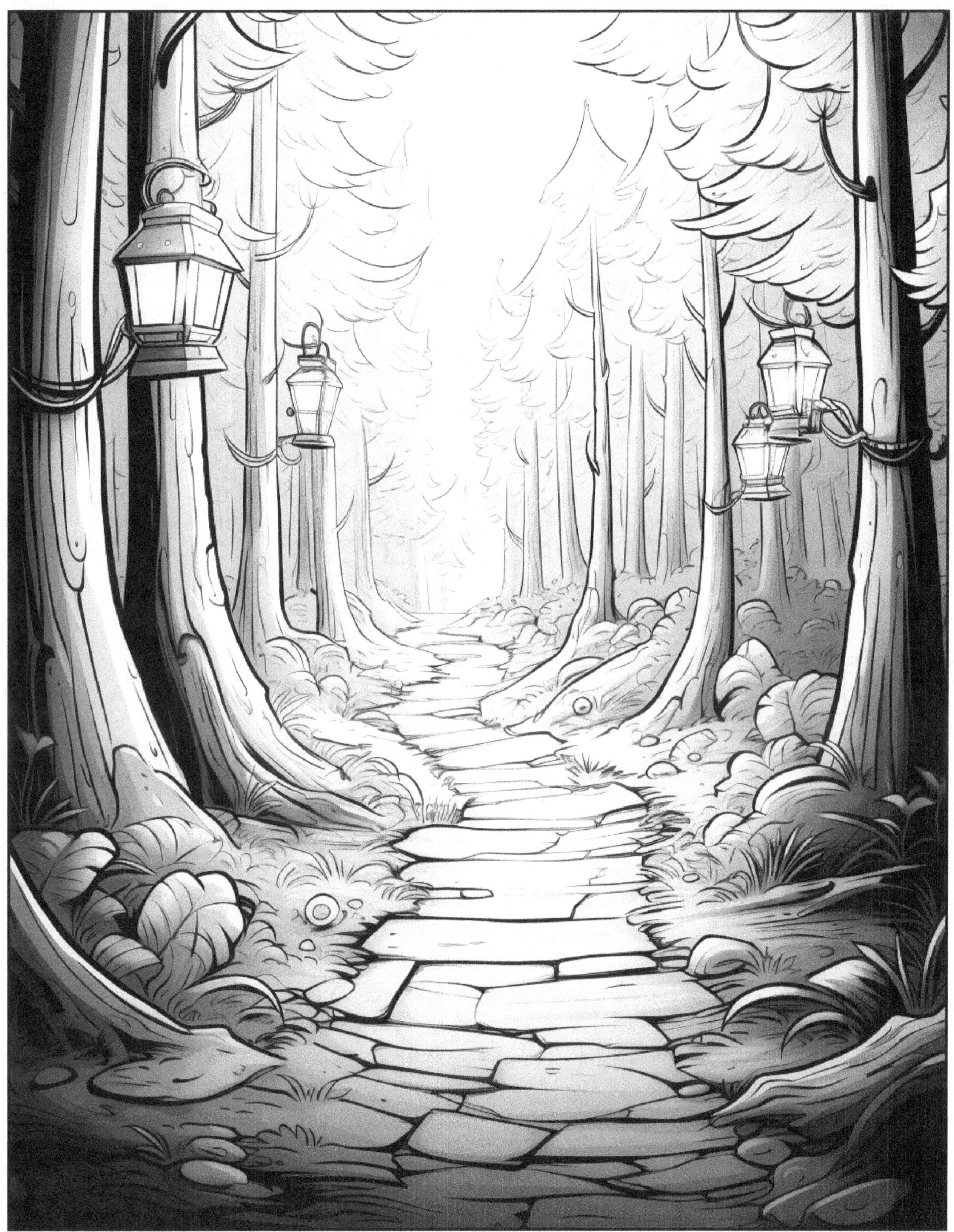

Wise tortoise so slow,
tales of old to bestow,
in the woods, a wise friend to know.

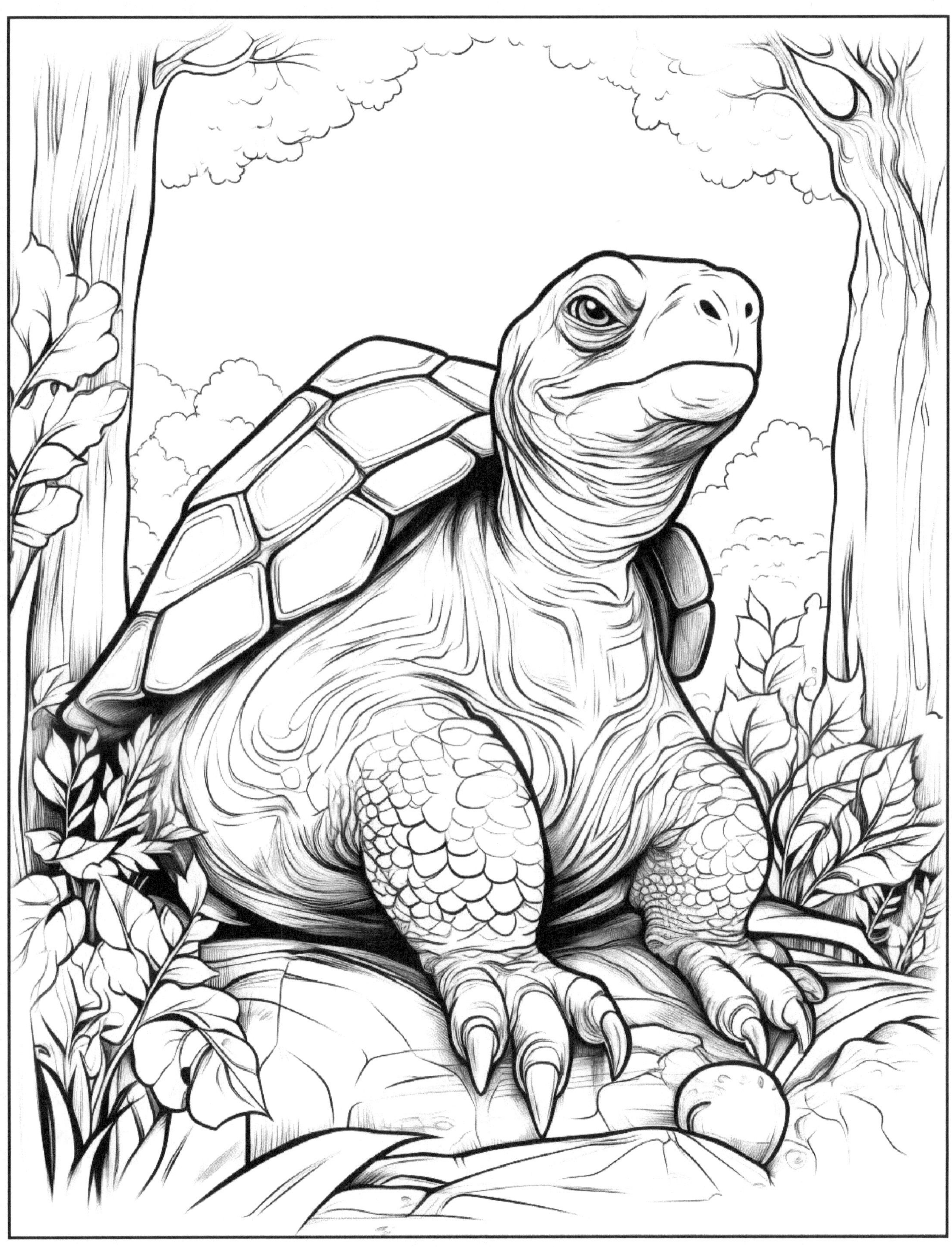

Tree with swings so high,
invites us to the sky,
in the woods, where dreams can fly.

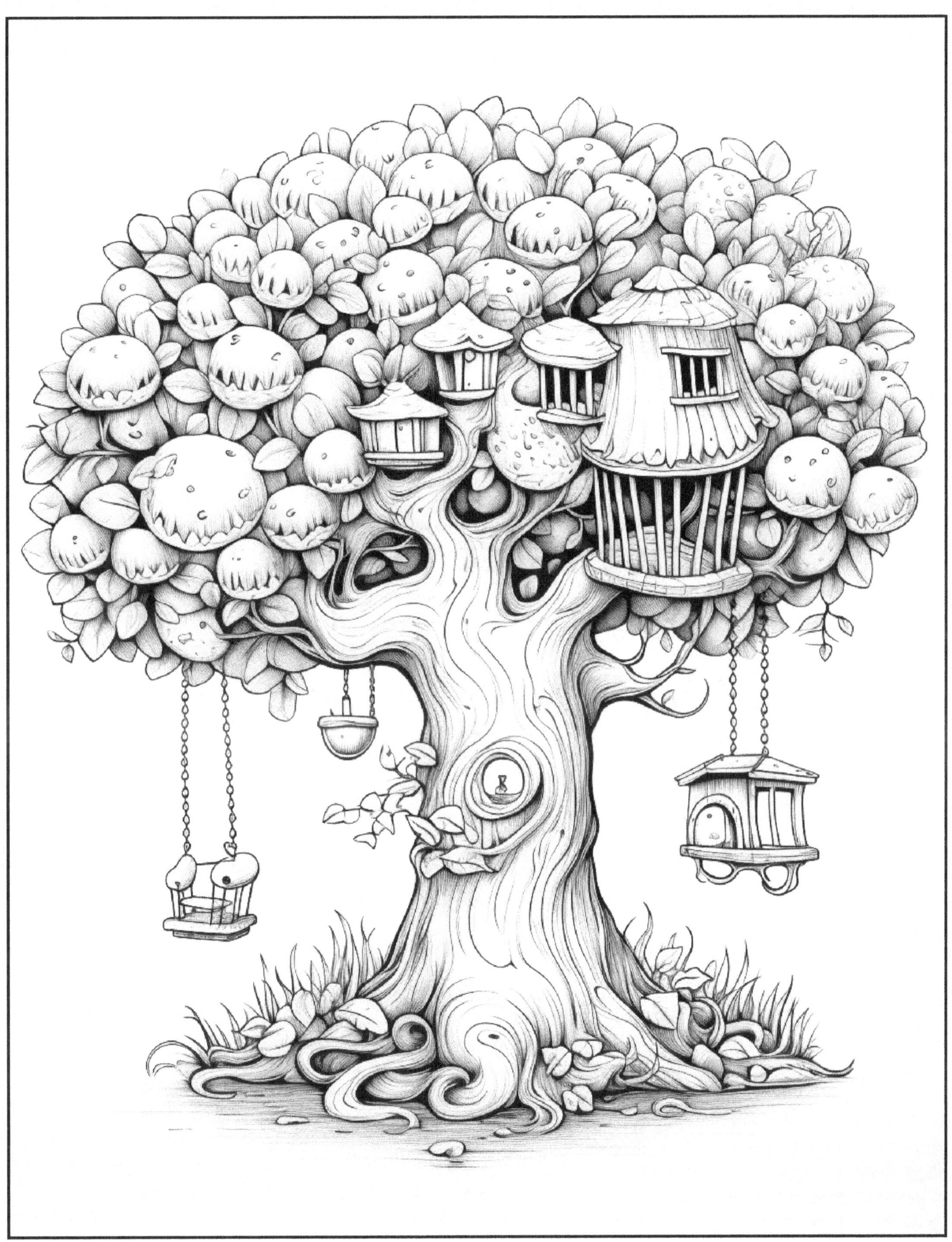

Baby owls learning to fly,
under the moonlit sky,
with their mother, so high.

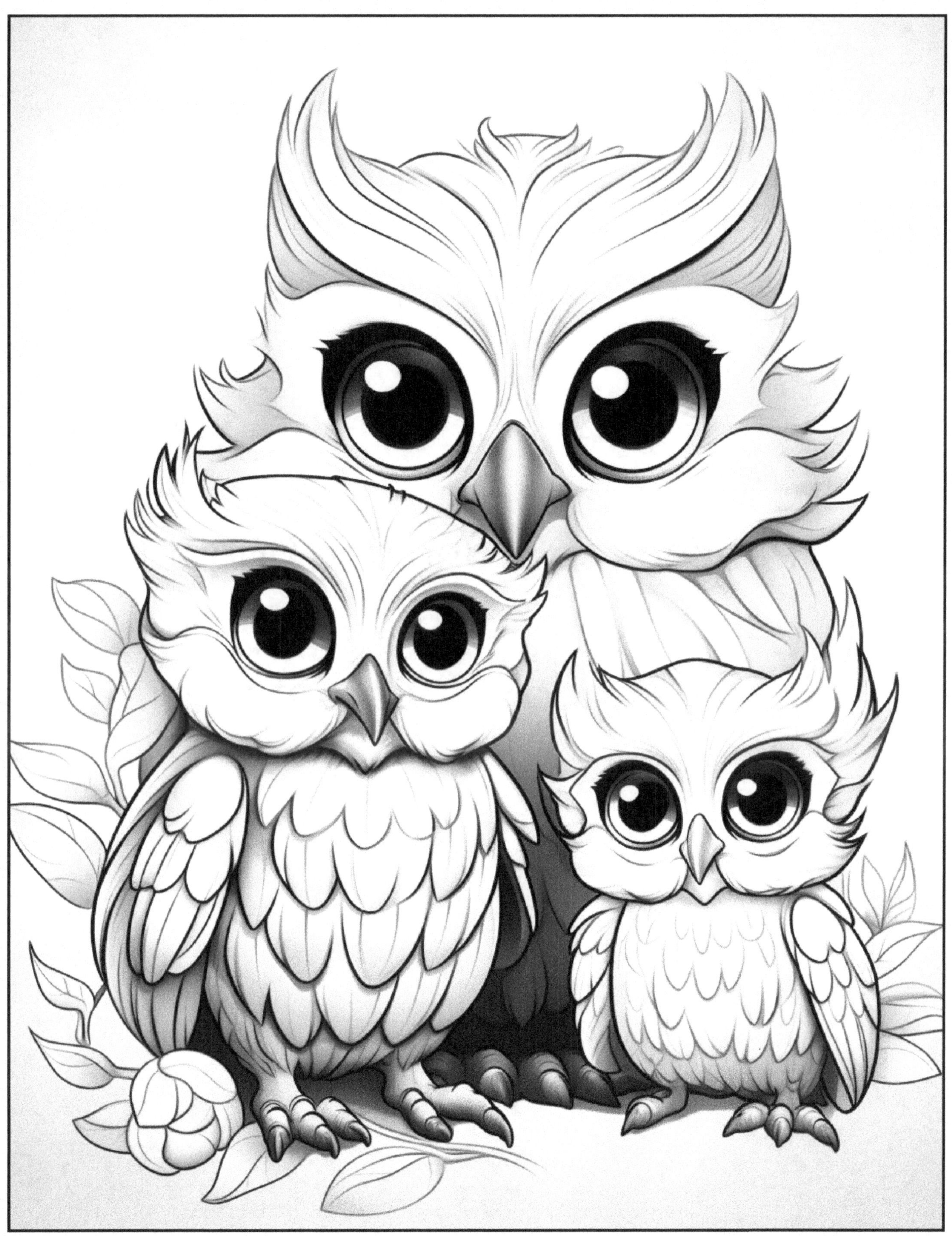

Peacock so grand and bright,
showing off colors so right,
in the meadow, a vibrant sight.

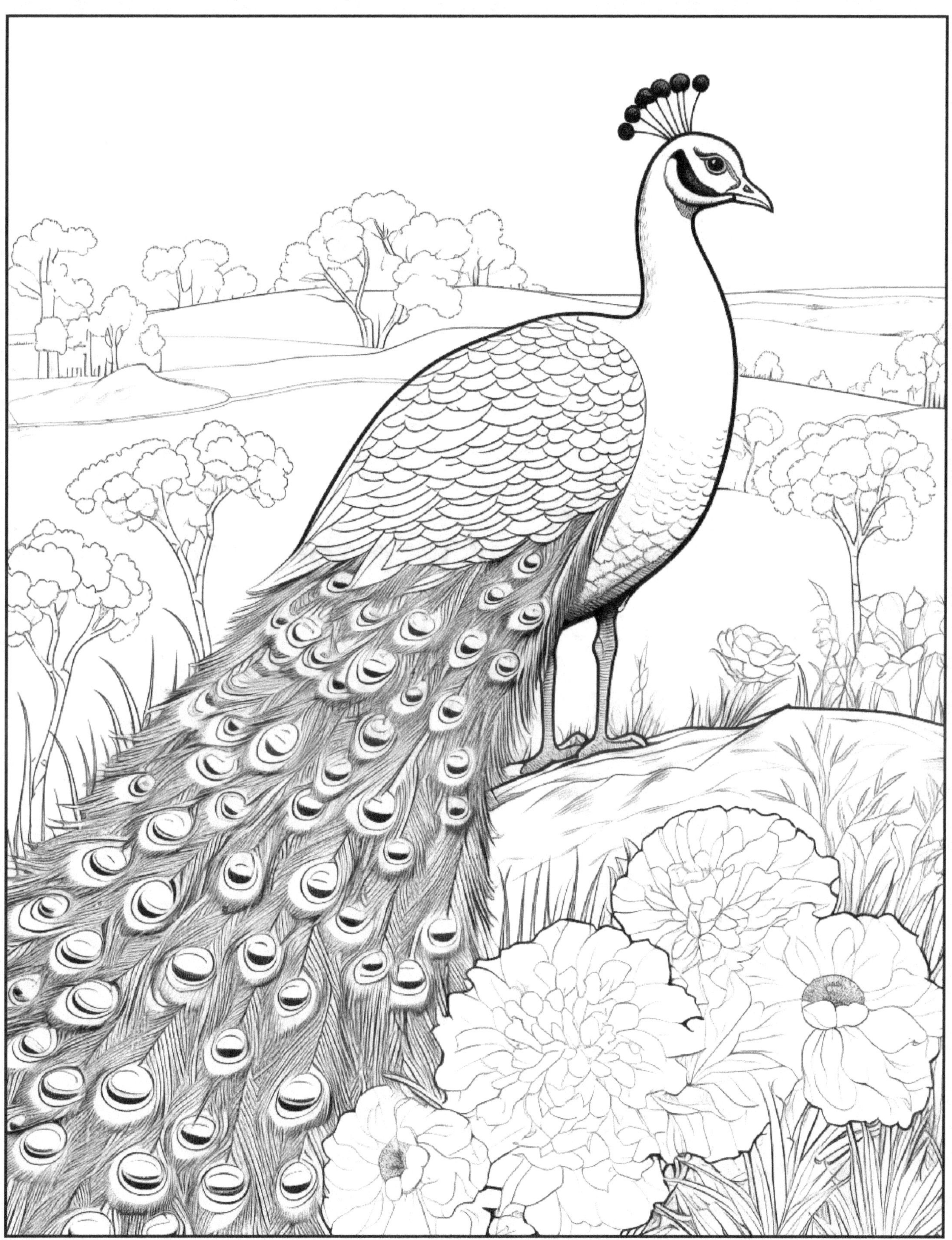

Firefly lanterns in the air,
like stars, glowing everywhere,
lighting up the night with flair.

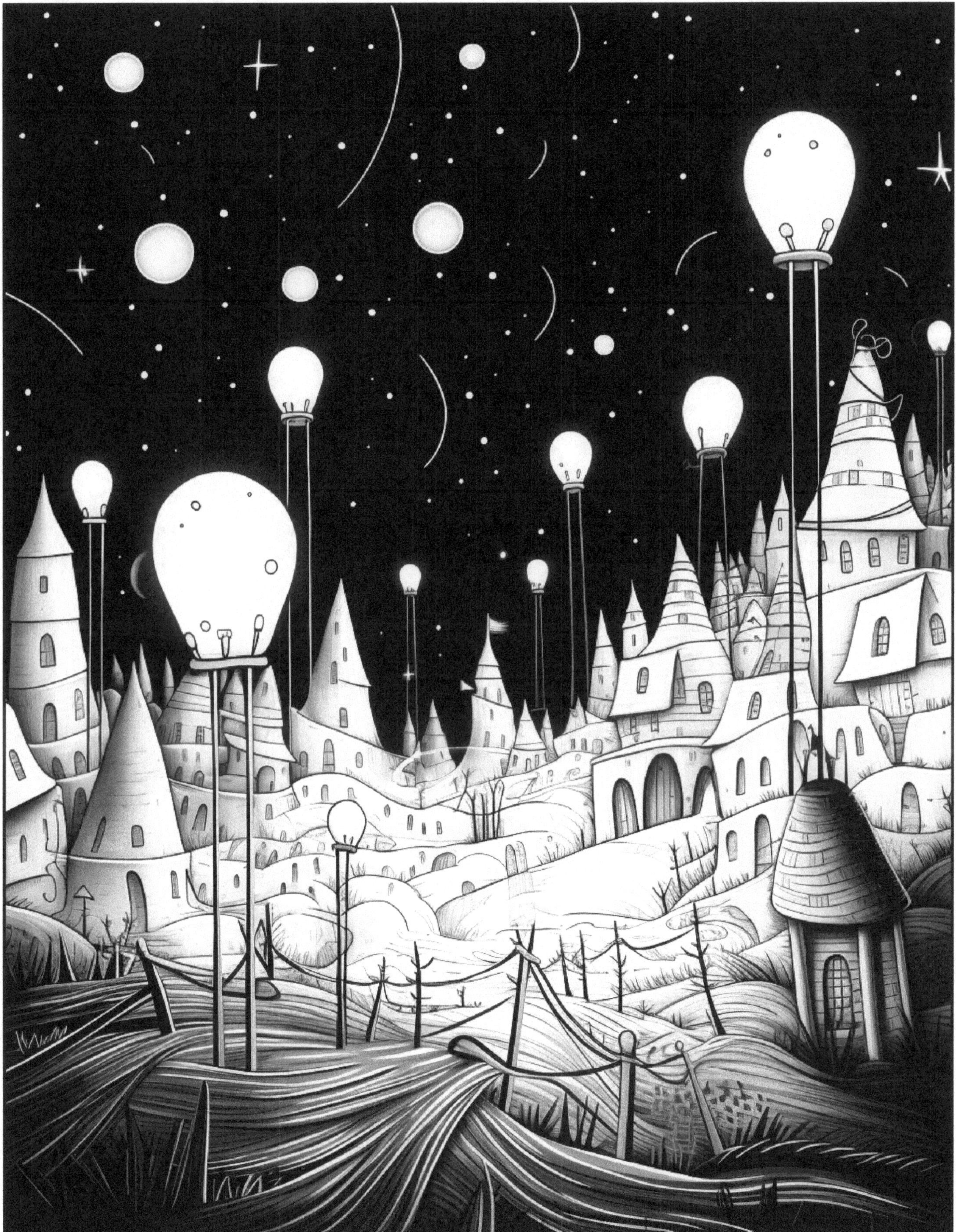

Badger leads the way, in a woodland
parade,
joy and laughter, never to fade.

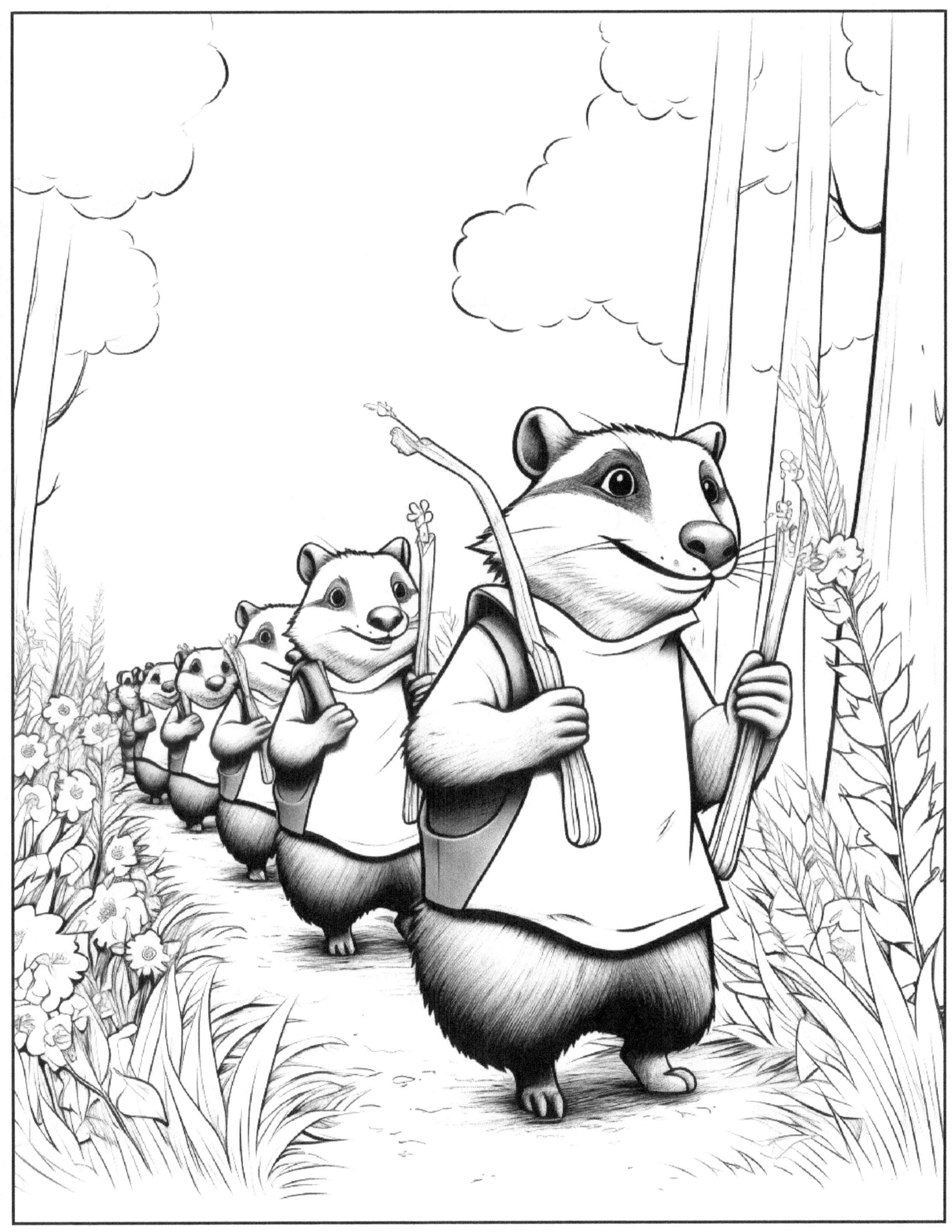

Campfire in the night,
warmth and light,
with woodland creatures, a cozy
delight.

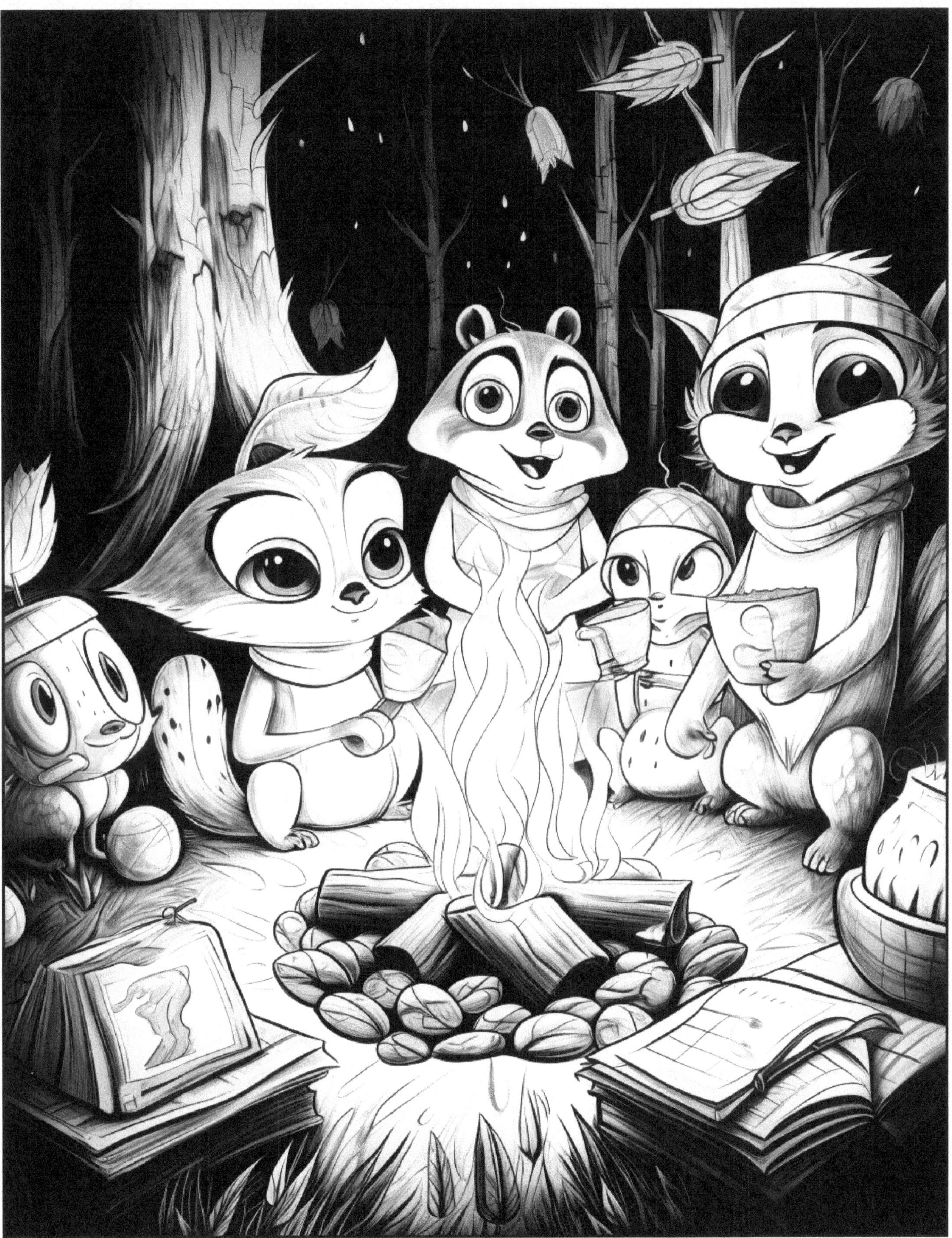

Cottage in the woods so small,
covered in ivy, a home for all.

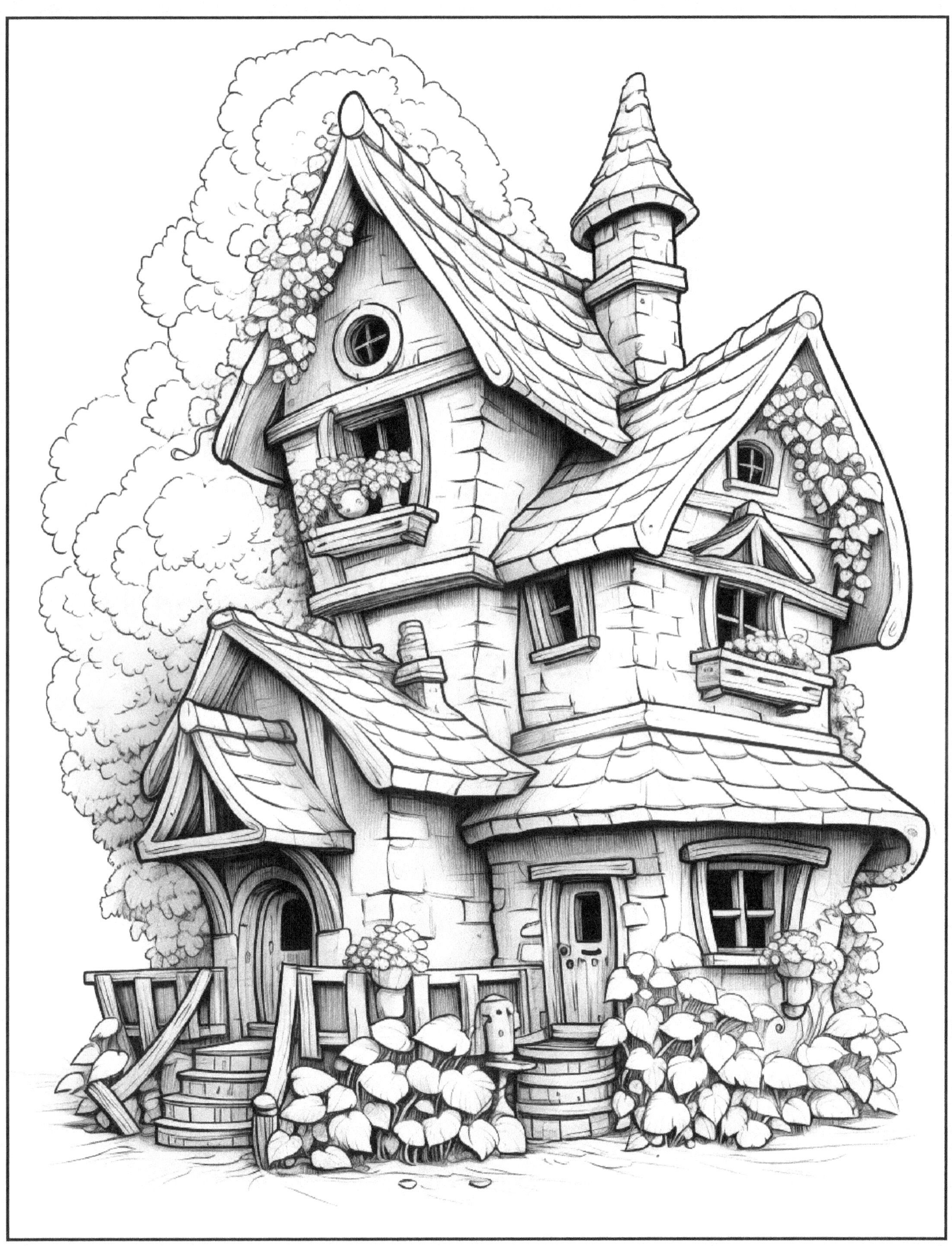

Mushrooms with smiles so bright,
in the woods, a cheerful sight.

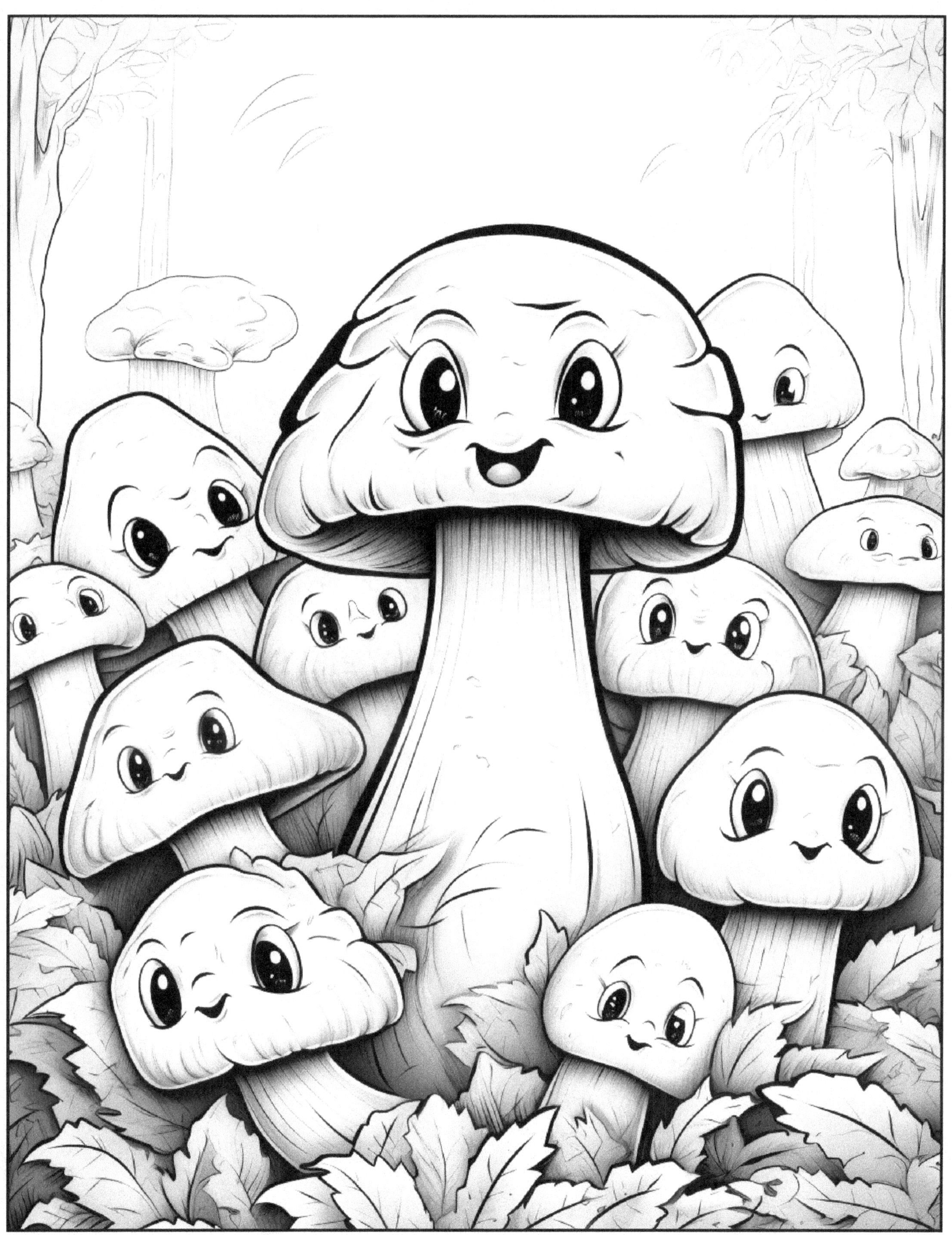

Beehive in the flowers' embrace,
buzzing bees in a lively space.

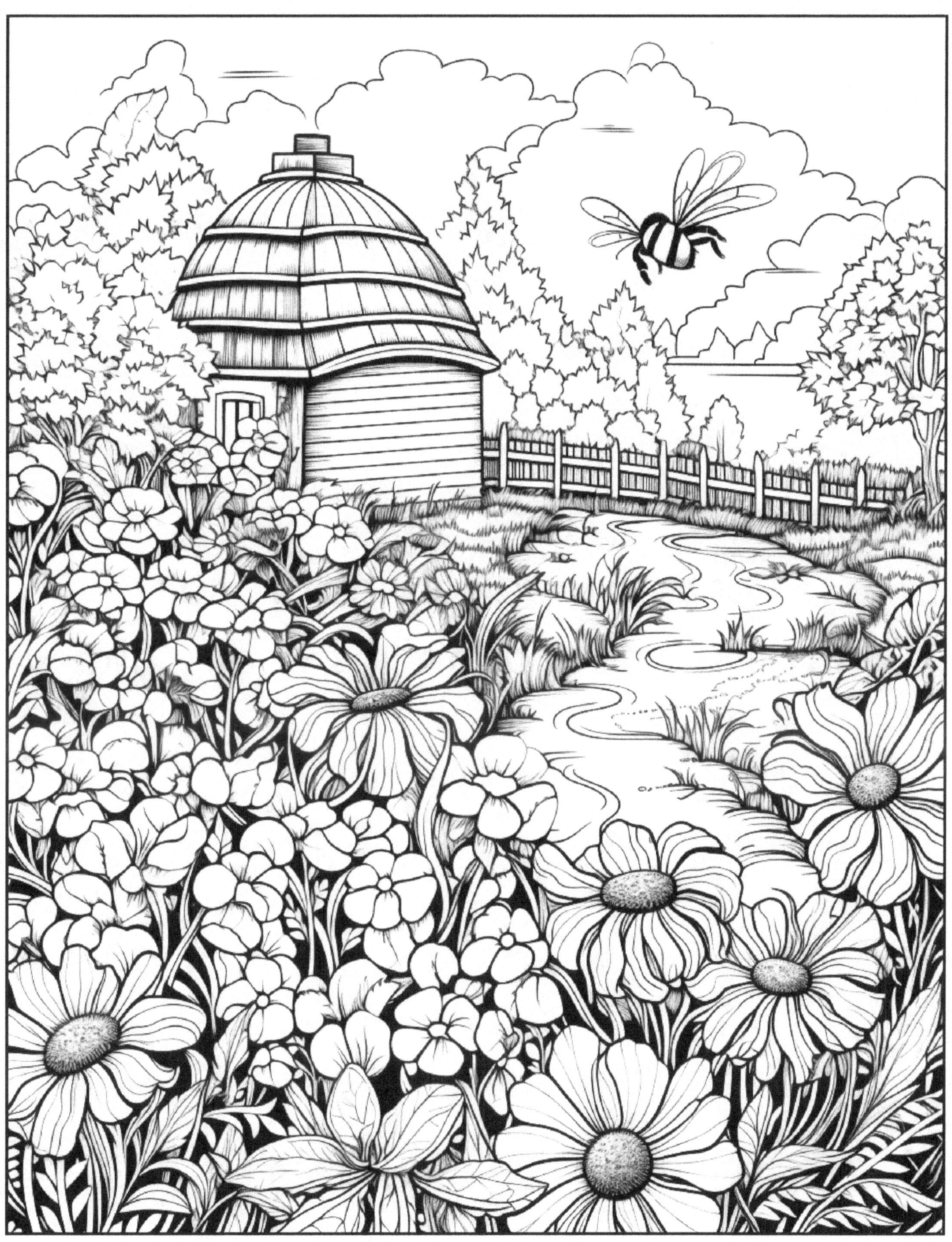

Pond so magical and grand,
with lilies and dragonflies, a fairyland.

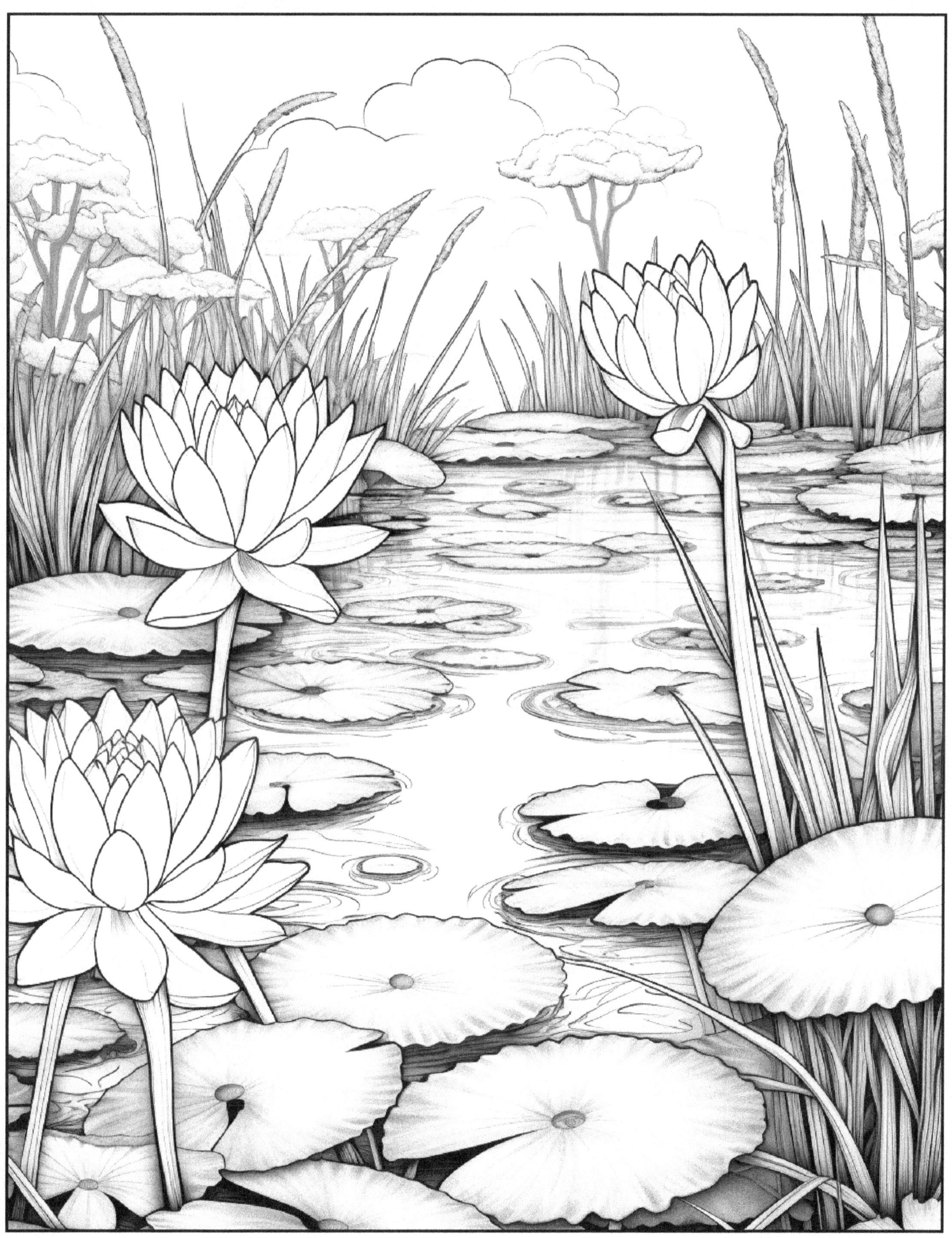

Frogs in a circle, having fun,
playing leapfrog in the sun.

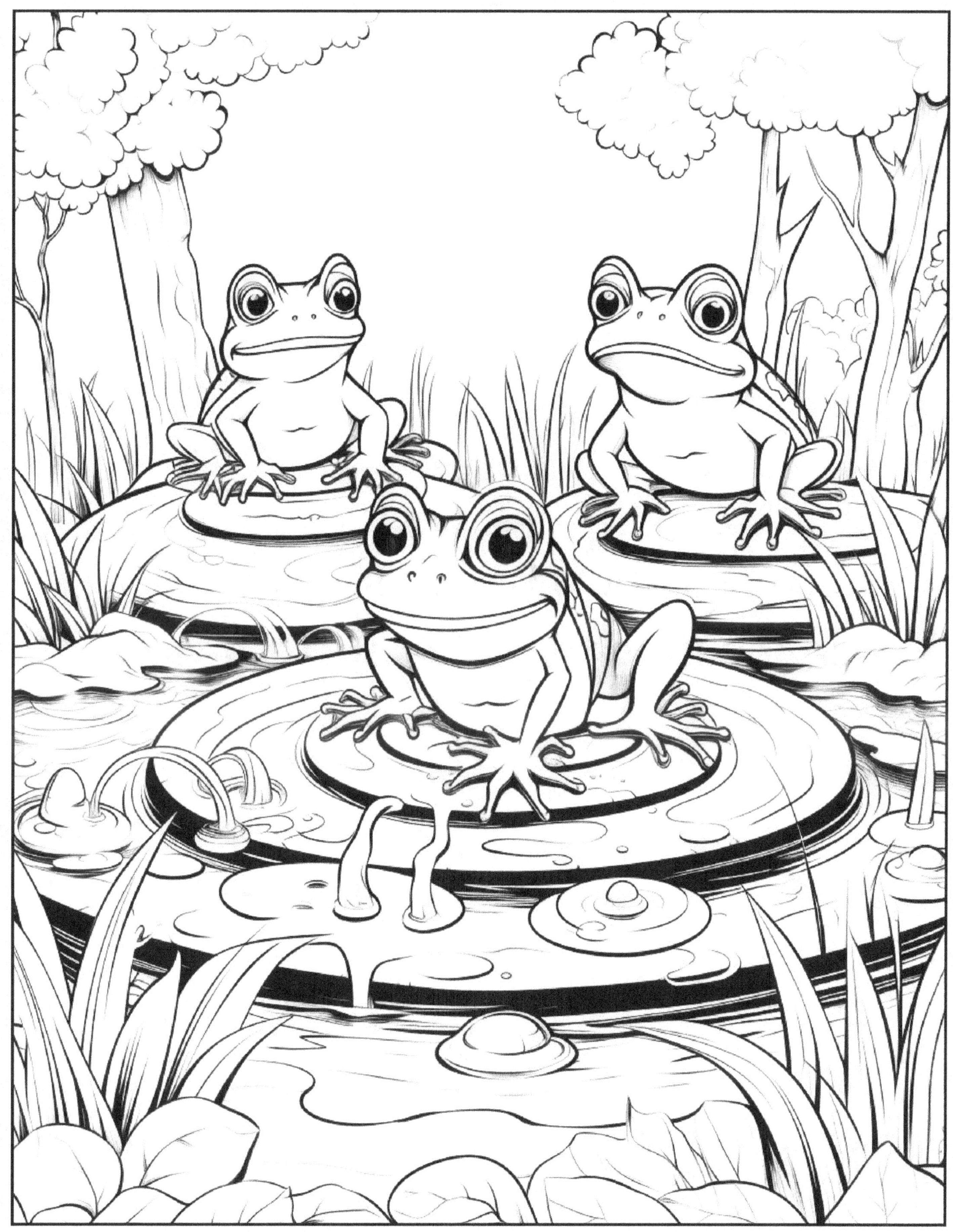

Rainbow bridge so high,
connecting trees to touch the sky.

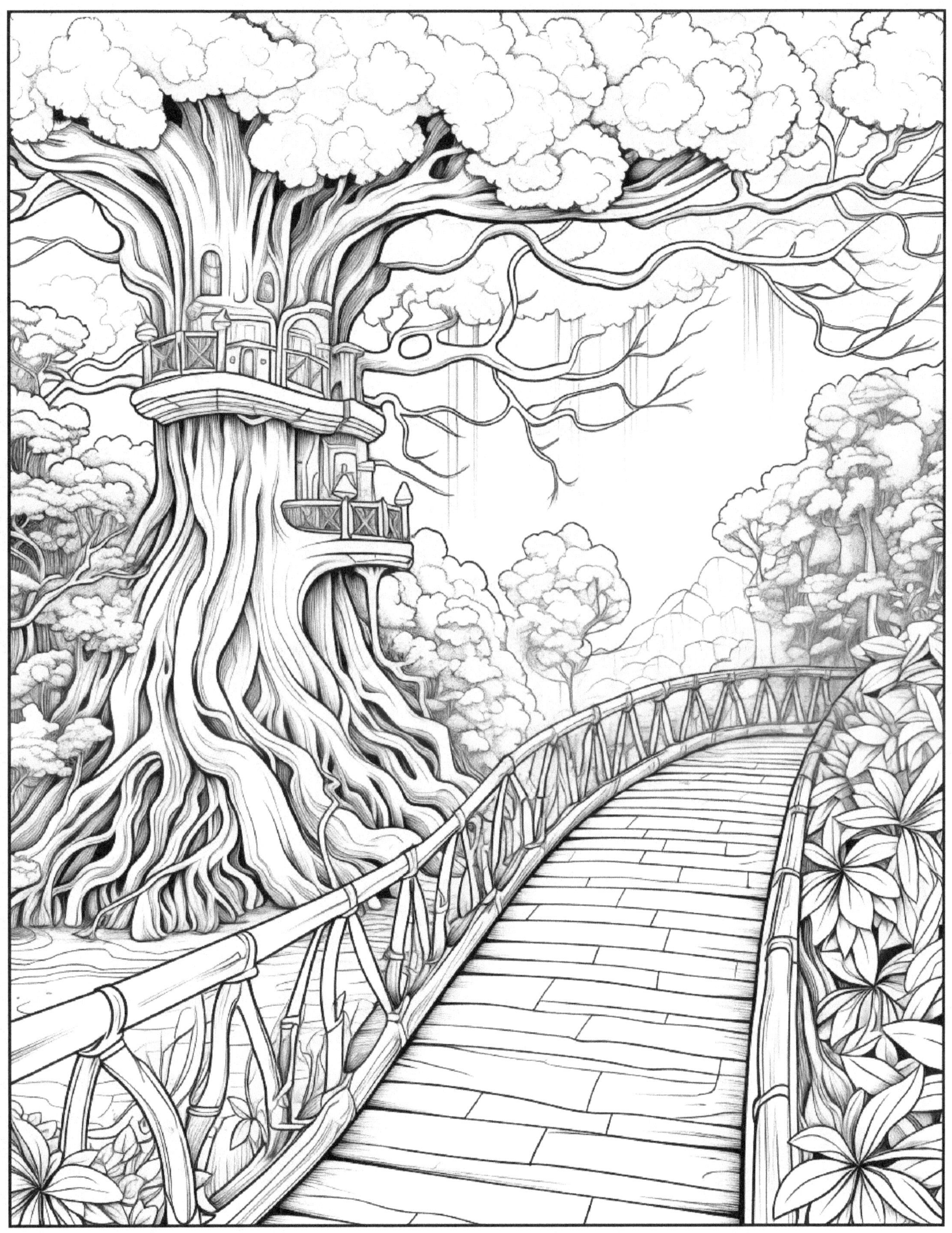

Snake in the mossy bed,
slithering friend with colors spread.

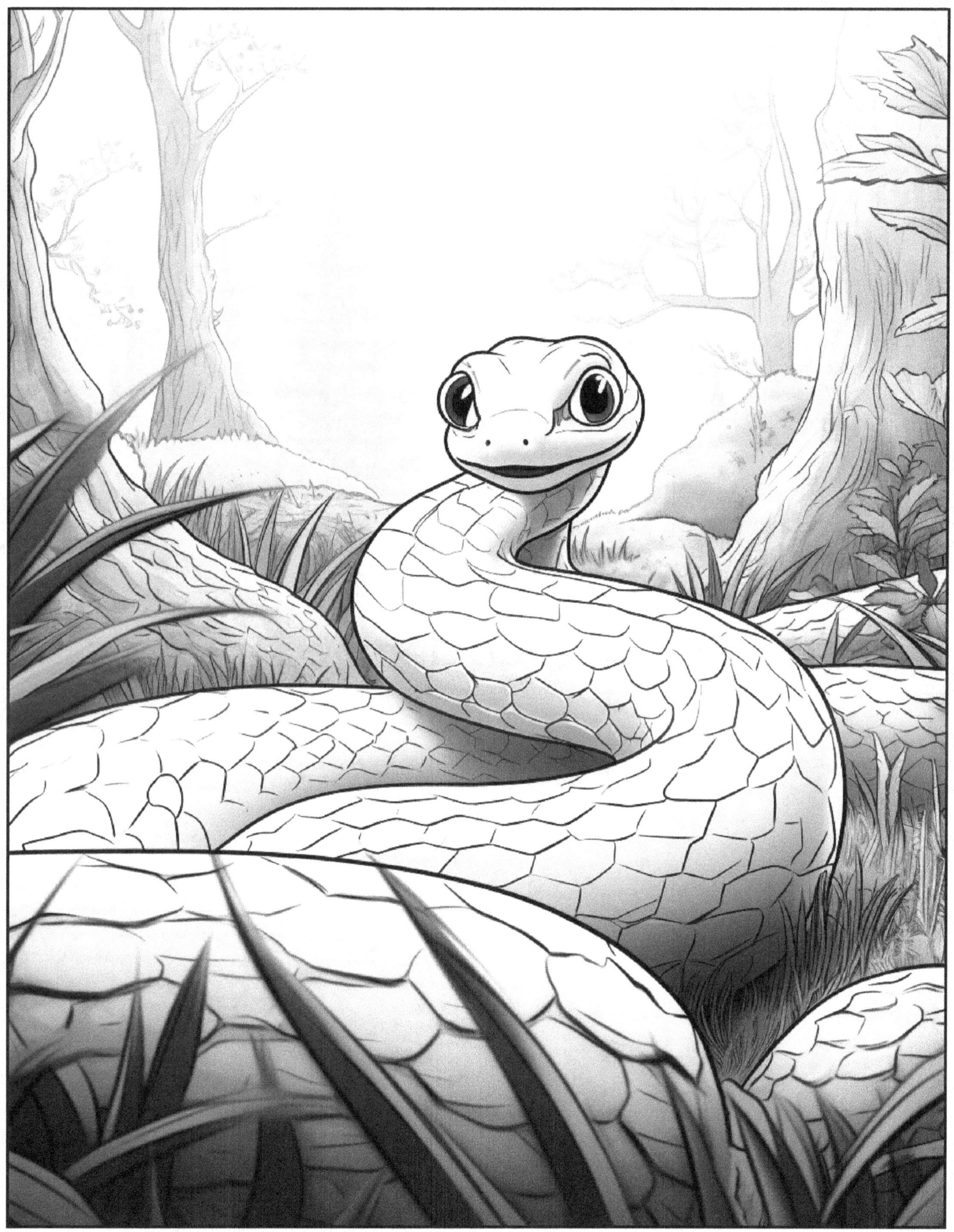

Sunflowers in the light,
faces shining, golden and bright.

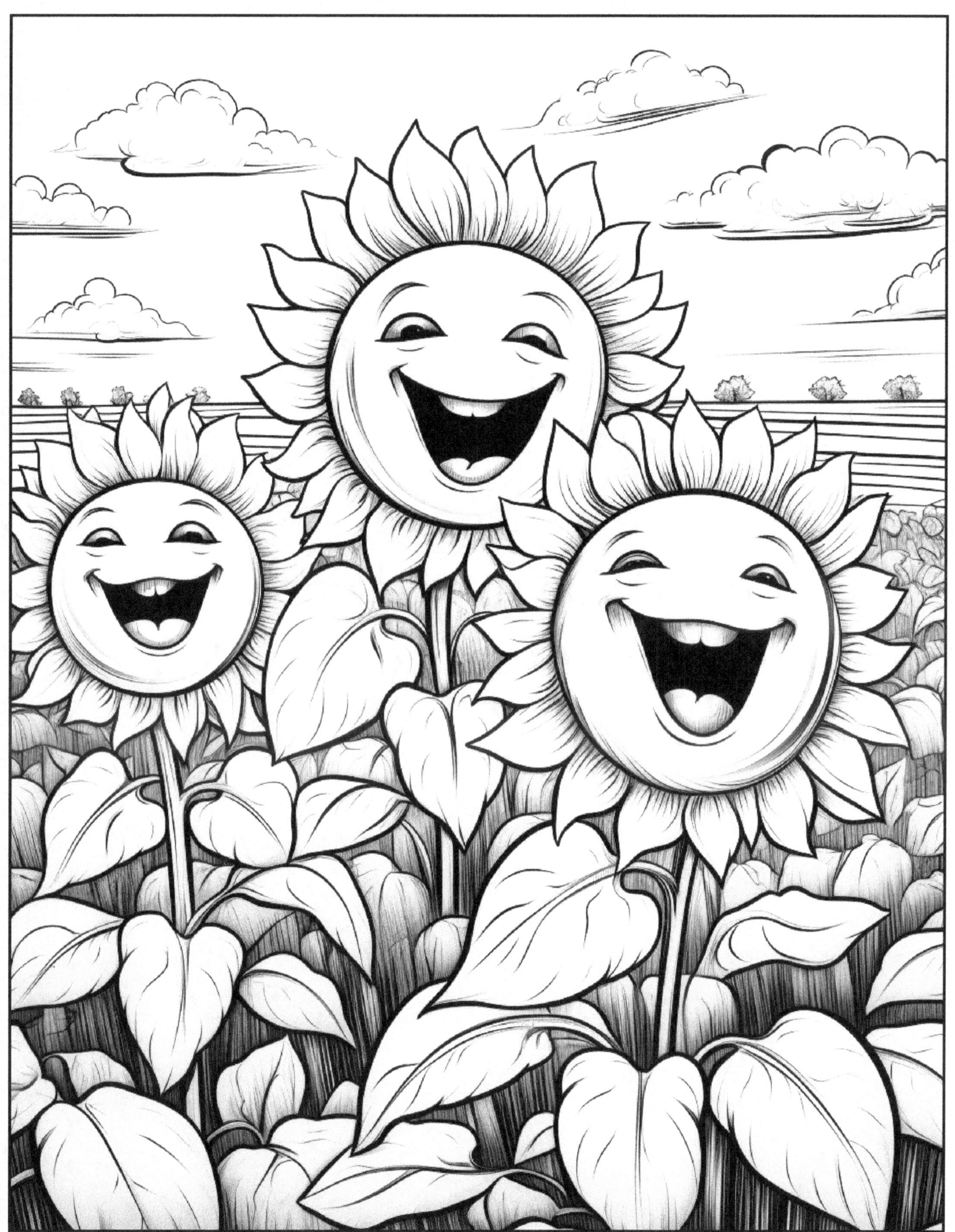

Old tortoise so wise and slow,
carries a lantern's gentle glow.

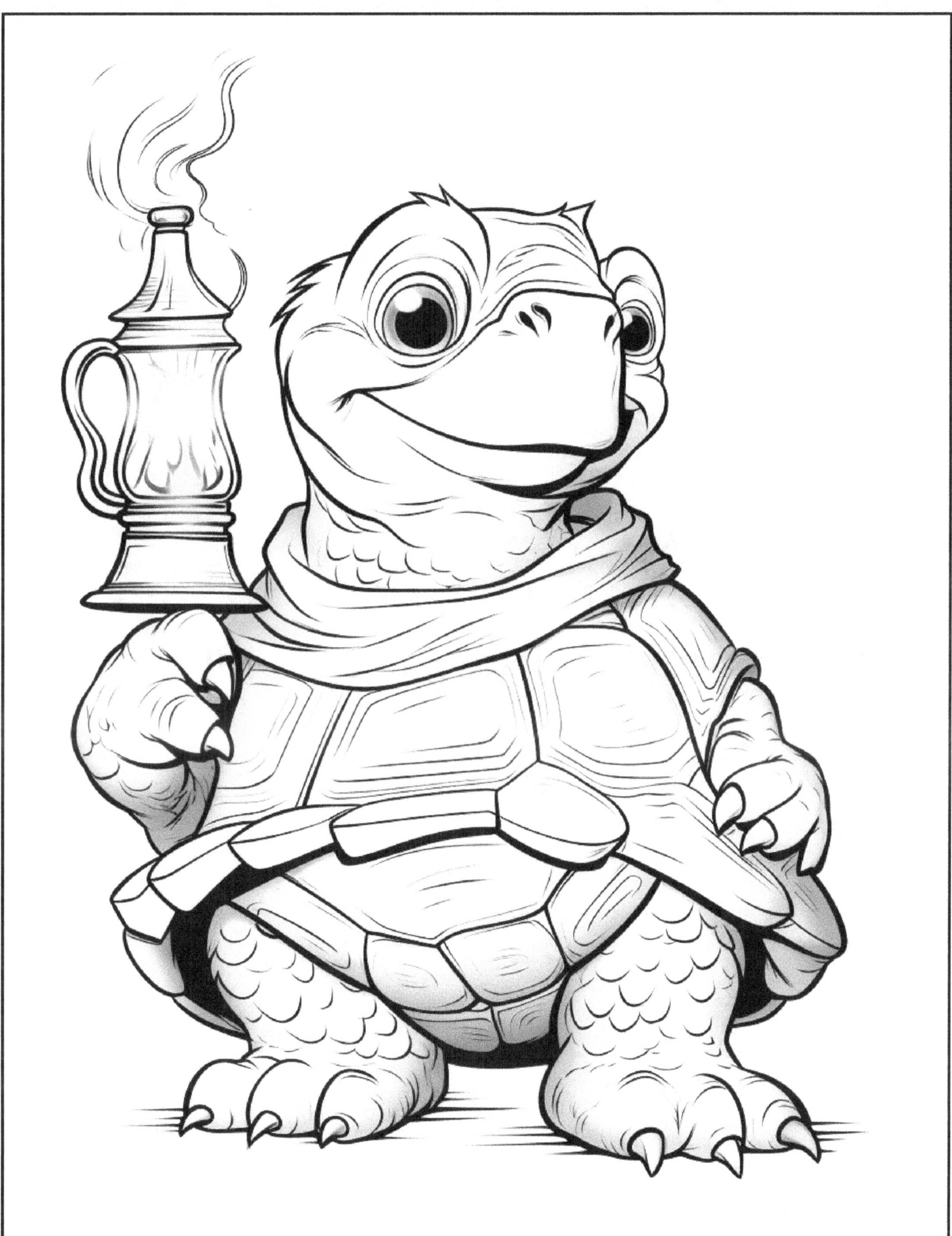

Ducks in the pond, a ballet so sweet,
surrounded by lilies, a graceful treat.

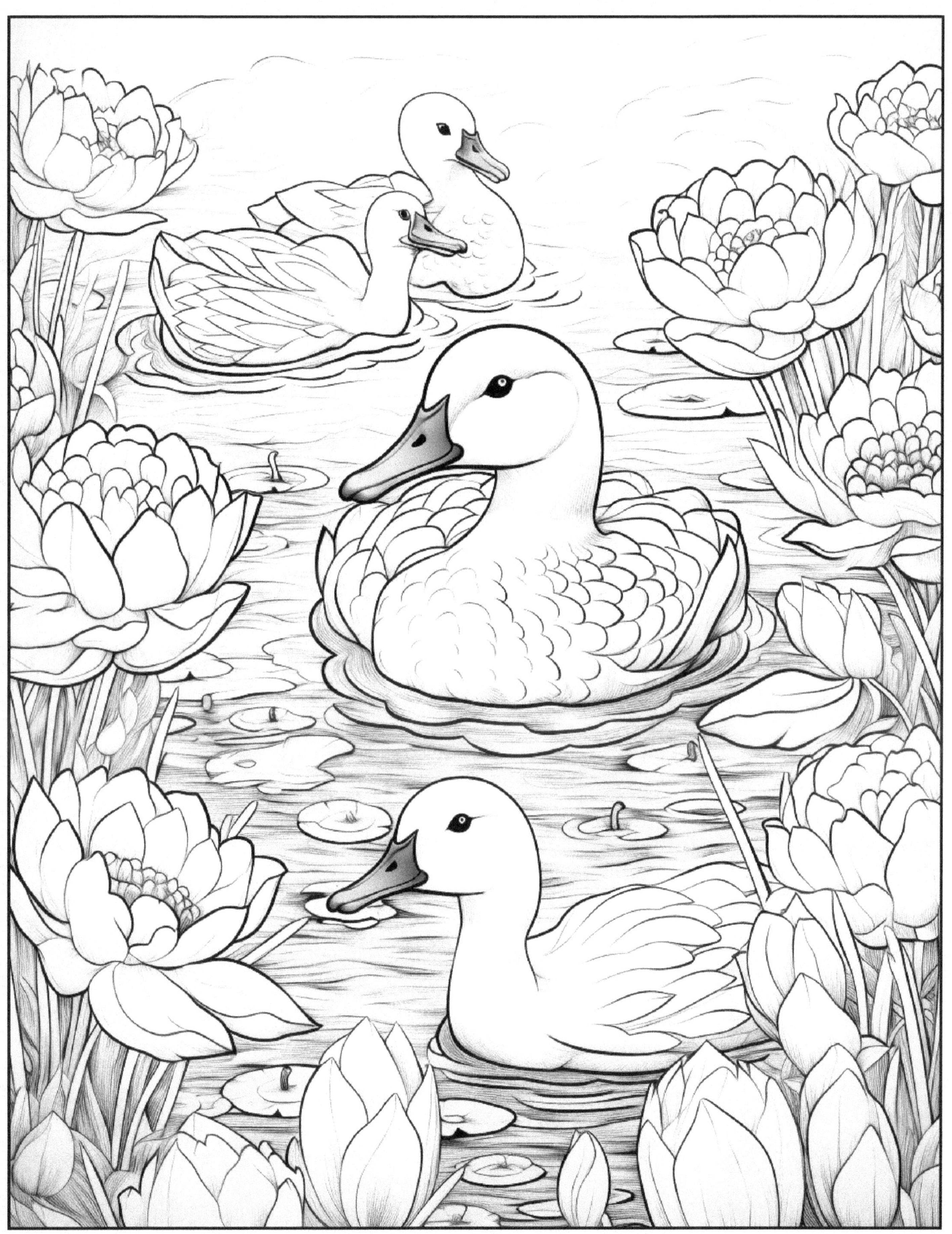

Lovebirds on a branch so high,
chirping sweetly, under the sky.

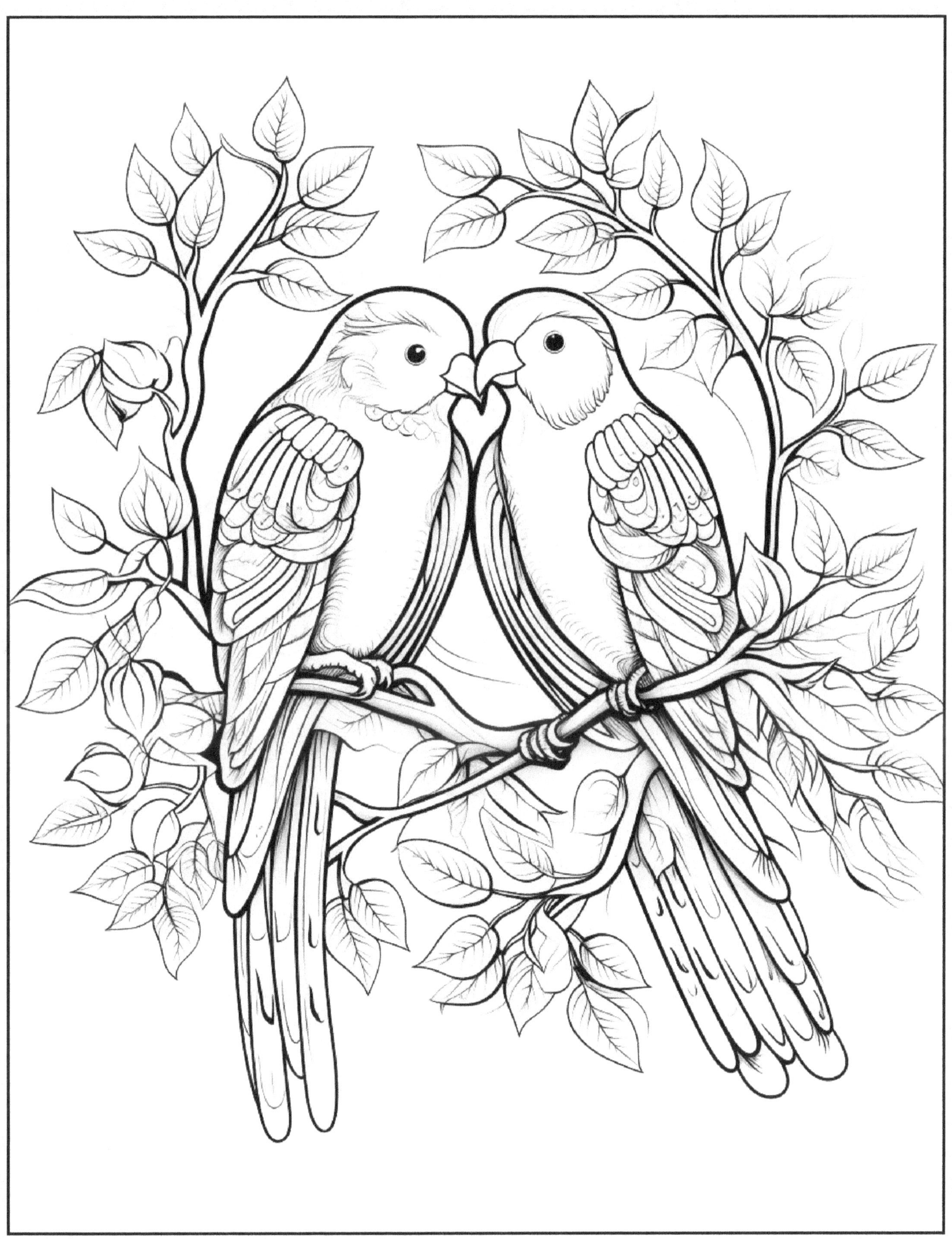

Toad with a tiny violin,
in a mushroom orchestra, plays tunes
so akin.

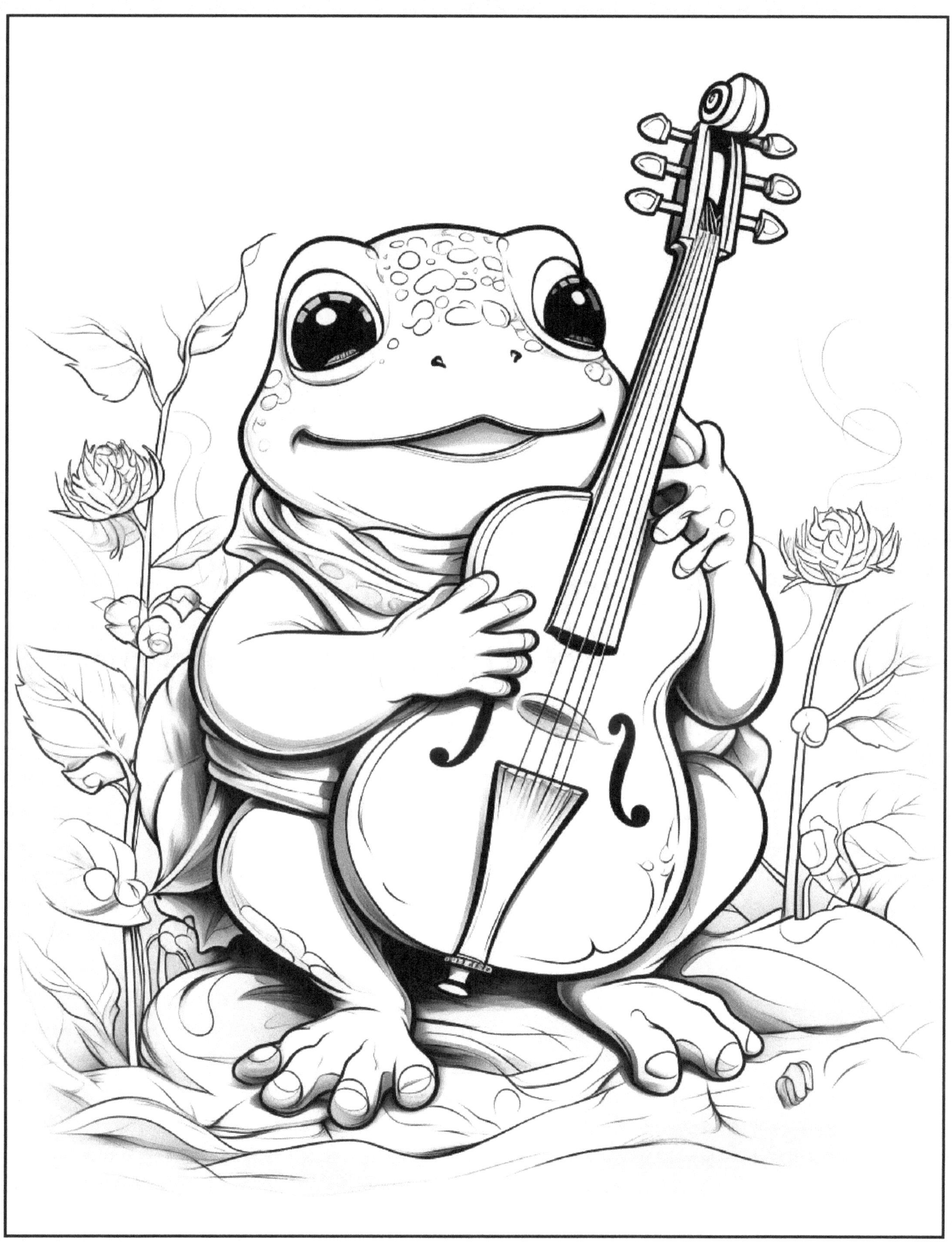

Butterfly garden in a colorful array,
flowers and butterflies dance and play.

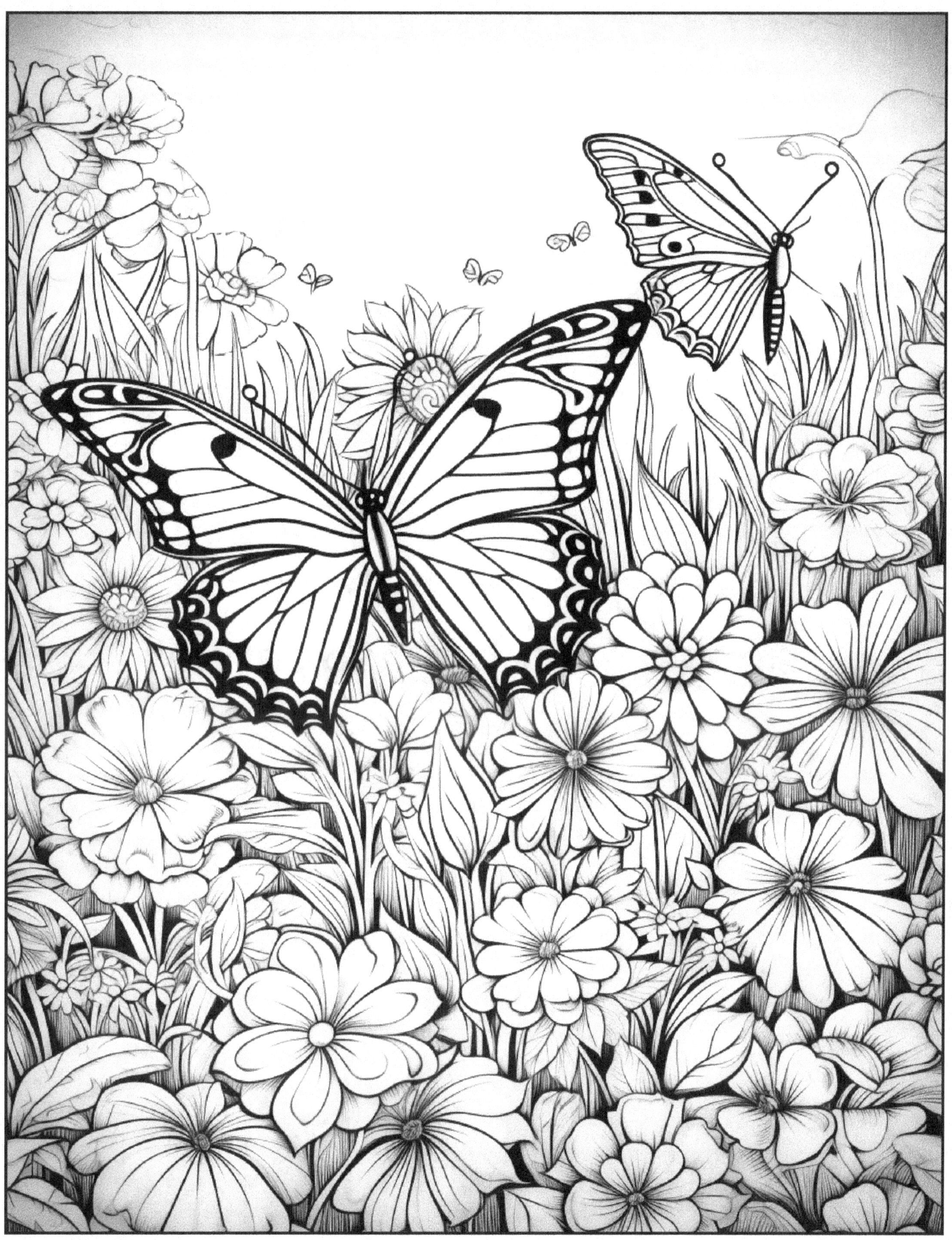

Hummingbirds in flight so small,
sipping nectar, a magical call.

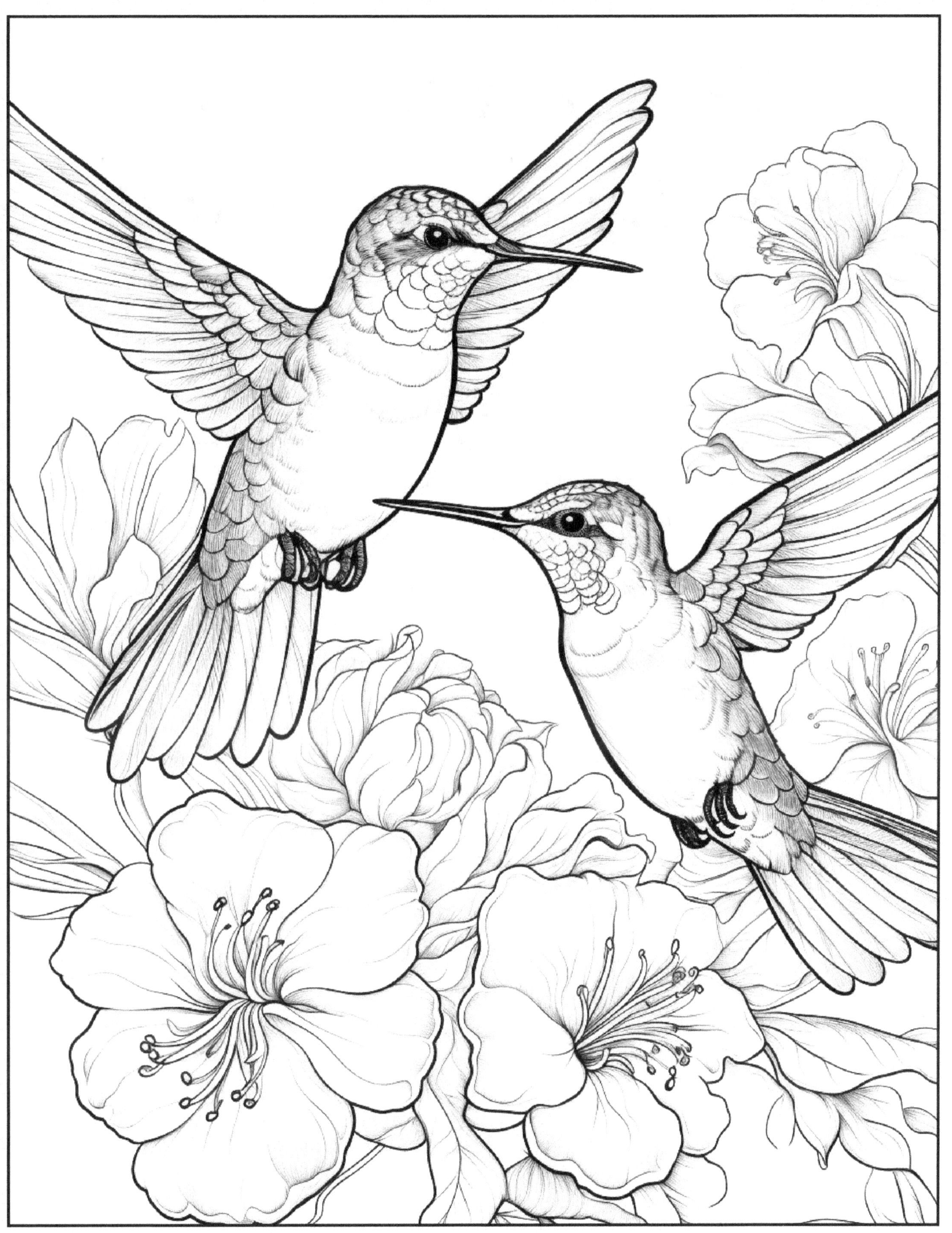

Your feedback is greatly appreciated!

It's through your feedback, support and reviews that I'm able to create the best books possible and serve more people.

I would be extremely grateful if you could take just 60 seconds to kindly leave an honest review of the book on Amazon. Please share your feedback and thoughts for others to see.

To do so, simply find the book on Amazon's website (or wherever you purchased the book from) and locate the section to leave a review. Select a star rating and write a couple of sentences.

That's it! Thank you so much for your support.

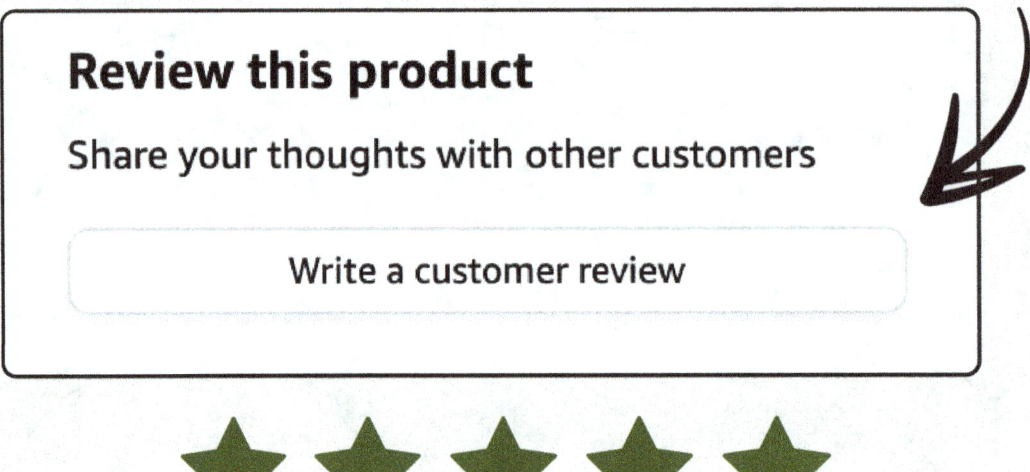